The Heart That Makes a Home is not simply a ...., ... process. In the next six weeks, you will make a journey that will propel you miles down the road toward being a more fruitful and accomplished wife. Each of the six video lessons is accompanied by a week's worth of devotional readings, prayers and Scriptures. And there's a lot of searching and growing to be done between lessons. So whether you start the process alone or as part of a group, we strongly encourage you to view just one of the video sessions per week – and let the course take its course in you.

Video Course Notes

In each session section, you'll find fill-in-the-blank questions that follow along with the video point by point. As you watch the video, write down key points and Scriptures. This is a vital part of the learning process, a way to make sure that you retain what you learn.

Video Discussion Questions

Throughout each video session, you will see a thought-provoking Discussion Question. Pause the tape at this point and plan to spend about 3–5 minutes on these questions as they appear. This will help each person in your group begin to own the principles presented.

Small Group Discussion Questions

Following the video course notes for each session, you will find a set of compelling questions to use for group discussion. These questions are designed to uncover the heart of each individual, and to expose your pre-existing beliefs. As you discuss your answers together in the group, you will quicken the process of transformation as you affirm and encourage each other.

Daily Devotionals

In between your weekly video lessons, these daily devotionals will challenge you to apply what you've learned to your life. Here is a wealth of wisdom and encouragement that is bound to be the highlight of your day.

Bible Studies

On pages 49 and 95, you'll find Bible Studies designed to cement the material you're learning during the week. Use these studies to focus on your role as the wife – you may even want to complete the studies with your husband and discuss the principles together.

Transformer Cards

Punch these perforated cards out of your book and put them in your pocket. With a prayer on one side and Scripture on the other, they are the touchstone you can always count on to help you become the wife God wants you to be. Each of the six lessons comes with two cards – one for morning and one for evening. Use the same two session cards every day for a week, and you'll begin to feel those verses sinking deep into your soul. And transforming all that you are.

The Heart That Makes a Home
TABLE OF CONTENTS

Transformer Cards for each session can be found in the back of this workbook.

Walk Thru the Bible presents

the HEART
That
MAKES
a HOME

BIBLICAL
WOMANHOOD
SERIES

DR. BRUCE H. WILKINSON

For more than three decades, Walk Thru the Bible has created discipleship materials and cultivated leadership networks that together are reaching millions of people globally through live events, print publications, audiovisual curricula, radio, television, and the Internet. Known for innovative methods and high-quality resources, we serve the whole body of Christ across denominational, cultural, and national lines. Through our strong and cooperative international partnerships, we are strategically positioned to address the church's greatest need: developing mature, committed, and spiritually reproducing believers.

Walk Thru the Bible communicates the truths of God's Word in a way that makes the Bible readily accessible to anyone. We are committed to developing user-friendly resources that are Bible-centered, of excellent quality, lifechanging for individuals, and catalytic for churches, ministries, and movements; and we are committed to maintaining our global reach through strategic partnerships while adhering to the highest levels of integrity in all we do.

Walk Thru the Bible partners with the local church worldwide to fulfill its mission, helping people "walk thru" the Bible with greater clarity and understanding. Live events and small group curricula are taught in over 50 languages by more than 60,000 people in nearly 60 countries, and more than 100 million devotionals have been packaged into daily magazines, books, and other publications that reach over five million people each year. And, in addition to our ever-expanding stock of newly created curricula, we have recently updated Walk Thru the Bible "classics" from every era of our history into digital formats. These resources, new and old, continue to bear fruit in churches, ministries, and individual lives throughout the world.

Walk Thru the Bible

Helper-Session 1

Introduction –*Attacking the role of the wife*

How do we know what it's like to be a woman? From TV? Other women? Our parents' example?

Biblical Passages on the Role of Helper

"And the LORD God said, "It is not good that man should be alone; I will make him a _____ comparable to him…. So Adam gave names to all cattle, to the birds of the air, and to every beast of the field. But for Adam there was not found a helper comparable to him." *Genesis 2:18, 20*

"So God created man in His own image; in the image of God He created him; male and female He created them. Then God blessed them, and God said to them, "Be fruitful and multiply; fill the earth and subdue it…." *Genesis 1:27-28*

Biblical Perspectives on the Meaning of "Helper"

1. Perspective #1: The one who _____.

"But I am poor and needy; make haste to me, O God! You are my help and my deliverer; O LORD, do not delay." *Psalm 70:5*

2. Perspective #2: The one who _____. (Psalm 10:14; Psalm 86:17)

"Fear not, for I am with you; be not dismayed, for I am your God. I will strengthen you, yes, I will help you, I will uphold you with My righteous right hand." *Isaiah 41:10*

3. Perspective #3: The one who _____. (2 Chronicles 14:11; 2 Chronicles 25:8)

"But the prince of the kingdom of Persia withstood me twenty-one days; and behold, Michael, one of the chief princes, came to help me, for I had been left alone there with the kings of Persia." *Daniel 10:13*

Discussion   *When your husband was struggling, how did you stand by your man?*

A. The _____ is our Helper.

"So we may boldly say: 'The Lord is my helper; I will not fear. What can man do to me?'" *Hebrews 13:6*

B. The _____ is our Helper.

"Nevertheless I tell you the truth. It is to your advantage that I go away; for if I do not go away, the Helper will not come to you; but if I depart, I will send Him to you." *John 16:7*

C. The _____ is our Helper.

"And I will pray the Father, and He will give you another Helper, that He may abide with you forever." *John 14:16*

Biblical Portrait of the Helper:

"By God's design, the wife is the helper of the husband and actively assists, encourages, and supports him."

Biblical Principles for the Helper:

1. The helper of the husband is the wife because of God's _____.
   (Genesis 2:18-23)

Discussion *Do you ever feel God favors your husband over you?*

"So God created man in His own image; in the image of God He created him; male and female He created them. Then God blessed them, and God said to them, 'Be fruitful and multiply; fill the earth and subdue it; have dominion over the fish of the sea, over the birds of the air, and over every living thing that moves on the earth.'" Genesis 1:27-28

A. *Principle*– Equality of _____, but Diversity of _____. (Genesis 1:26-27)
"And the LORD God said, 'It is not good that man should be alone; I will make him a helper comparable to him.'" Genesis 2:-18

B. *Pattern* – The woman is _____ to the man. (Genesis 2:18-23)
"For man is not from woman, but woman from man. Nor was man created for the woman, but woman for the man." 1 Corinthians 11:8-9

C. *Priority* – The woman is _____ the man. (1 Corinthians 11:8)

D. *Purpose* – The woman is _____ the man. (1 Corinthians 11:9)

E. *Perfection* – The woman is the _____ to the man. (Genesis 2:18-23)

1. Can you name several examples of "helper" as depicted in popular culture?

_____

_____

_____

_____

2. How do these examples differ from God's idea of "helper"?

_____

_____

_____

_____

3. What are some ways you act as your husband's helper?

_____

_____

_____

_____

4. How would you rate yourself as your husband's "helper"? How would your husband rate you?

_____

_____

_____

_____

5. What is the biggest obstacle that keeps you from fulfilling your position as "helper"?

_____

_____

_____

_____

BACK TO SCHOOL
WEEK 1, DAY 1

Genesis 2:18 —

"And the LORD God said, 'It is not good that man should be alone; I will make him a helper comparable to him.'"

"Pam, could you give me hand with this please?" came the voice from the study. Keith was trying to reconcile the bank statement before leaving on a business trip. And of course he couldn't get anywhere without Pam's help.

"Honey, I said *just a minute*!" she responded. "Now, where was I?"

Pam was sorting through the loot she had collected from a week's worth of back to school shopping. And as anyone who knew Pam could tell you, she prided herself in keeping all her ducks in a row, especially when it came to the children. If anyone enjoyed being organized, it was Pam. And with only hours to go before the big day, she was relishing the challenge.

"Three pairs of size 4 jeans... and three in size 6... I just know I had another blue shirt when I got to the register...."

The book bags were piled beside the door, full of fresh supplies and ready to go. Notebooks, pens, pencils, erasers, folders, and a personal organizer for each child, to help them keep it all straight.

"Paaaamm," came the faint plea again.

"Hold on!" she assured him. "There it is! I knew that shirt had to be here somewhere!"

Pam finished organizing the remaining items into neat stacks. Then she began the final task of counting the inventory one last time. There were matching shirts and pants, shorts and play clothes, socks and shoes, jackets, lunch boxes, key rings, and locks for lockers...

"Pam?"

"Just a *second*!"

Was there anything she was overlooking?

WEEK 1, DAY 1

From the Word

Apparently Pam was forgetting just one thing – her husband Keith! There can be many duties that fall on the wife's shoulders. But none is more important than her first calling: to be the helper to her husband. Scripture provides a clear sense of order for all aspects of life. It's not that the other responsibilities are not important. It's just that when several things are competing for first place, God wants us to elevate the husband to the top priority.

For the heart

When you, as a parent, send a child off to school, there's a sense in which everything you do is focused on the mission of helping your child succeed in his new environment. Your antennas are up, making sure all the bases are covered. God wants us to have the same focus toward our husbands in everyday life. How about you? Do you wake up each morning committed to the mission of helping your husband succeed? Do you view life through the lens of *How can I be his helper?* Are all your activities organized around this primary objective? Or do you sometimes let other responsibilities crowd him out? Maybe it's time to "go back to school," and re-examine God's primary purpose for the wife.

There's a fine line between a job well done and a job, well... done.

EQUAL RIGHTS
WEEK 1, DAY 2

Genesis 1:27-28a—

> *So God created man in His own image;*
> *in the image of God He created him; male and female*
> *He created them. Then God blessed them...."*

The Ladies' Night Bible Study hadn't been so energized in all their ten years of meeting together. When they invited the guest speaker to lead a study on the role of the wife, they had no idea how controversial it could become. After the lecturer was introduced, she quietly stepped to the microphone and uttered a single statement for her opening remark.

"The wife's job is to help the husband," was all she said. Then she asked the women to gather in small groups and share their responses to that statement. She would give her speech afterward.

The room was quiet and orderly as they began. One by one, the women went around their respective circles sharing their opinions. As they did, a low din began to fill the room. Gradually, it swelled to a controlled racket. And finally... bedlam.

"Most abuse begins with that same type of thinking!" threatened one woman.

"But it says right here that Sarah obeyed Abraham *without a word*," said another, attempting to repeat a point from a recent Sunday school lesson.

"God never intended for the woman to be lorded over," someone exclaimed.

"Sure, the wife should help... but the husband should help too," said another.

All over the room, the responses formed a swell of diverse opinions and strong emotions. Some suggested that the statement could be found in the Bible. Others said it was a first-century philosophy. There was no sign of agreement anywhere in the room.

Through it all, the speaker sat quietly at the front of the room and smiled as the group passionately demonstrated her first point: The role of the wife is unclear today, even among Christian women.

WEEK 1, DAY 2

From the Word

When it comes to the role of the wife, the world seems more confused than ever. And much of the confusion can be traced to a common misunderstanding about the "helper." The Bible is clear that God made the woman to be "a helper comparable to him." But many women mistake that assignment as a demotion. While God gave man and woman different roles, He made them equal in status... He "blessed them" equally. When the wife assumes the role of helper, it is no more of a demotion than when a highly trained physician helps a sick patient. It's simply a role assigned by God.

From the Heart

God is the highest of all beings, and He Himself chose to assume the role of helper. So it goes without saying that the wife is in a special category when she agrees to be the helper to her husband. Where do you stand on this issue? Have you cleared up all confusion about your role? Do you resist the role of "helper," viewing it as the equivalent of a slave-girl? Or do you see it as a way to reflect God's love by sharing in the role He chose for Himself? Are you free to be your husband's helper, first and foremost? It may not be the most popular choice with some women, but it's pretty popular with God.

In a Godly marriage, help is only a heartbeat away.

HELP THAT HELPS
WEEK 1, DAY 3

Luke 14:28—

"For which of you, intending to build a tower, does not sit down first and count the cost, whether he has enough to finish it...."

"John, I need you to take the kids," Mary blurted as her husband stepped through the door from the garage with his briefcase.

"Take them where?" he asked, trying to size up the situation.

"Nowhere... anywhere... just *take* them! I just need a break...."

John looked around the room and quickly got the picture. There were crayons and papers scattered across the kitchen table. Bags full of groceries were stacked on the counters, still waiting to be put away. A pot of unidentifiable food was boiling over on the stove. And the faint sound of whining children echoed from the playroom upstairs.

Mary retreated to her bedroom and sat down on the edge the bed in the same spot where she had begun the day with her morning devotions. She'd had such high ambitions for the day. She had planned to cover so many of her weekly errands. She had stimulating activities in mind for the kids. And more than anything, she intended to have her husband's favorite meal on the table when he walked through the door at the end of the day. But now she just felt so defeated. Anger, frustration, and stress brewed inside. She didn't know whether to be angry at herself, at God, or at the Proverbs 31 woman who seemed to have started this whole fiasco with her "Wonder Woman" standards. Mary meant well. She wanted to manage the house smoothly and be a help to her husband. But it seemed like the harder she tried, the worse things got. Where did she go wrong?

WEEK 1, DAY 3

From the Word

In our accomplishment-oriented society, we wives can be guilty of measuring our success based on how many "Christian" things we accomplish in a day. If it is virtuous to do a good deed, then it must be more virtuous to do a hundred, right? And if you really want to be a Christian wife, then you'd better keep a "Proverbs 31 list" and check off each item every day, right?

Not necessarily. All throughout Scripture, God's Word reminds us of the importance of wisdom and prudence. Following God is not so much about *doing* things as it is about doing the *right* things at the *right* times. Whenever God calls you to a task, He provides a method and a plan for accomplishing it. Our Creator is the God of many monumental achievements, but He is also the God of peace and order.

For the Heart

What about you? Do you ever rush into the day with a "more is better" attitude? Or do you stop to consider a strategy that's best for the overall picture? Sometimes the key to accomplishing *more* is trying *less* – that which is *manageable*. You can push yourself to the limit "helping" your family. But it can quickly reach the point where *you* need help instead. Perhaps it would be better to try just one or two things in a day. You'll not only enjoy the sense of accomplishment, but you'll be prepared in the event of a setback.

A true "helper" steps back and asks, "What is *truly* helpful to my husband?" God called you to be the wife of your husband, but He called you to be His child first. Don't forget to build time into your day for slowing down and listening for His voice. Sensing His presence throughout the day will cultivate the fruit of His Spirit in you. And that can be nourishing for everyone in your family!

If you want more peace, *try smaller* pieces!

THE MISSING LINK
WEEK 1, DAY 4

1 Corinthians 11:11—

"Nevertheless, neither is man independent of woman, nor woman independent of man, in the Lord."

Susan could hardly believe the words that were coming out of her own mouth. She wasn't really thinking about a trial separation from Tom, *was she?*

Her mother leaned across the kitchen table, "Now calm down," she assured her. "Let's talk about this."

Susan reminded her mother of how they had almost called the wedding off because she wasn't sure they were meant for each other. Susan had a clear picture of where she wanted to go in life. She knew just what she wanted her family to be about. But Tom just seemed to drift along in life, without any clear goals. Susan used to believe they could make it work anyway. But now it seemed like the longer there were married, the more frustrating it was for her. She didn't know how much longer she could take it.

"Have you ever focused on really following Tom?" her mother asked.

"Follow Tom?! Follow *what?* He doesn't *lead*!" scoffed Susan. "Mom, Dad is so much more purposeful than Tom... I just don't think you can relate to what I'm going through. Face it, I married the missing link!"

Susan's mother took her by the arm. "Susan, he's not the missing link. *You* are."

"What are you talking about?"

Her mother went on, "*You* are the key to his success. I'll have you know that your father was not always the mission-oriented man that you see today," she began. "In fact, it used to drive me crazy how aimless we felt as a family."

"No way! Dad?" Susan exclaimed, "Well what happened?"

Her mother thought for a moment, "I'm not sure, exactly. Little by little, he just seemed to find himself. Tom's not that different from your Dad, Susan. I just believe that somewhere inside that man is another man waiting to come out. But he can't come out until it's safe."

"*Safe?*" Susan pressed. "What does *that* mean?"

"He needs your help," she explained. "It's your job to let him know that he always has your support... no matter what. He needs his partner."

WEEK 1, DAY 4

From the Word

In our culture, there is a strong tendency to approach marriage from the perspective of what you get *out* of it, rather than what you put *into* it. For the most part, people are willing to put something into a marriage as long as they get something back. But when they don't get something in return, they find it difficult to keep giving and giving.

Unfortunately, that approach fails to embrace God's design for marriage. God did not design man and woman simply to *support* each other, He designed them to *complete* each other. The wife must not approach marriage as a mutual agreement in which two people reap certain benefits from each other related to their skills, talents, and personalities. Instead, she must make it her driving passion in life to become the perfect complement to that man. She must see herself as the elusive, all-important, final piece of the puzzle.

For the Heart

Few things frustrate a woman more than trying to follow man that won't lead. At the same time, nothing frustrates a man more than trying to find his purpose in life without the help of his "completer." Whether he realizes it or not, he may never reach his full potential without your help.

How about your husband? Is there another man somewhere deep inside that's just waiting to come out? Is there something you could be doing to help your husband blossom into the man God created him to be? Write down at least one way you can "complete" your husband today. And put that final piece of the puzzle in place.

If your husband is only half the man you dreamed of,
you could be holding the other half!

THE MAIN THING
WEEK 1, DAY 5

John 21:22—

"Jesus said to him, 'If I will that he remain till I come, what is that to you? You follow Me.'"

The conversation was getting heated between Kim and her friend Judy. Judy tried to be gentle and encouraging, but Kim's emotions about her marriage were starting to get the best of her.

"But what if I go along with what he says and be his helper and he still doesn't change?" Kim pleaded.

Judy paused, searching for just the right words. Kim had finally hit upon the telltale question. *What if* it didn't work?

For the past three years, Kim's husband Joseph had been going through some personal struggles. His career was changing, his ambitions were changing... it seemed like his whole personality was changing. Kim had tried everything she knew to help him snap out of it, but nothing seemed to work. Now she was desperate. She was willing to try almost anything. Except, maybe she wasn't ready to try Judy's suggestion.

"I mean," Kim went on, "wouldn't I just be encouraging him to continue down the wrong path?"

Finally, Judy spoke. "Maybe it's not the wrong path after all, Kim."

"What? Are you kidding?" Kim looked despondent.

"Wait a second," Judy continued, "hear me out. Maybe this is the path he has to go down to find out where he really needs to be."

Kim lamented, "But if he'd just listen to me, it would save us all so much grief!"

"But that's not your job, Kim," Judy pressed. "Our job is to be a helper to our husbands... to be the one person who believes in him, especially when it seems unbelievable. If we don't do our job, then it just prolongs the struggle. Trust me, Kim, I've been there."

Helper–Daily Devotional

From the Word

Should Kim trust Judy? Maybe the deeper question is, "Should Kim trust God?" One day Jesus was talking with Peter and touched on this principle. Jesus had just revealed that the road ahead would not be easy for Peter. In response, Peter essentially asked, "But what about John?" Jesus quickly reminded Peter that he shouldn't be concerned about what God has in store for others… all of Peter's energy would be needed to make sure he was following God himself.

The same is true for the wife. It's easy to become focused on what our husbands should be doing or not doing. If you're not careful, you may find yourself wrapped around the goal of changing your husband. But that's a goal God reserves for Himself. And if that's your focus, then you're probably neglecting your own God-given goal: to be your husband's helper.

For the Heart

No matter what's going on in your husband's life, ultimately it's between him and God – whether he's a Christian or not. That doesn't mean you should leave him alone to figure it out. But it does mean you should trust that God will move in his life at the appropriate times. Meanwhile, you should be busy following God's call on your own life – to support, encourage, and *believe in* whatever God is doing in your husband's life.

How have you been doing in this area? Have you ever showed less than your full support for your husband? When he shares his dreams, do you play "Devil's Advocate" or do you look for ways to validate him as a man? You may not trust Judy; you may not even trust your husband; but you can always trust God!

You're not just helping your husband, you're helping God help him!

Helper-Session 2

Introduction—What does it mean to be the "Helper"?

Biblical Principles for the Helper (continued)

2. The Helper prioritizes her energies to help her _____.

A. The key priority is her husband, not her work, ministry, or _____.

"We wives are to put our husbands first, to take care of them and please them. This principle doesn't mean that we sit at home like doormats waiting to be stepped on. It does not mean that we don't have an original thought of our own. It means that we put our husbands first, before our children, before our parents, before our friends, and before our activities."– Florence Littauer

B. The key recipient of her help is her _____.

C. The key evaluator of the effectiveness of her help is her _____.

"The hostess poured a cup of tea for a middle-aged man at her party and asked him if he took sugar. 'No,' he said. 'Yes,' said his wife brightly at the same moment. Then she turned accusingly to him. 'But I always put sugar in your tea!' 'I know,' the man replied. 'I used to remind you not to. Now I just don't stir.'"

"You women may not like the fact that God made us to be helpmates for our men, but that's what God says, and He means business. We have to ask ourselves, 'Am I really a help to my husband, or would he be better off without me?'"– Florence Littauer

Discussion   *What do you do that really frustrates your husband?*
          How could you end his frustration?

"That they admonish the young women to love their husbands, to love their children, to be discreet, chaste, homemakers, good, obedient to their own husbands, that the word of God may not be blasphemed." Titus 2:4-5

3. The Helper is the divinely designated _____. (Titus 2:5)

A. Greek *oikos* means "home" and its " _____." (Titus 2:5)

"... the home is the extension of his wife's personality, not his. The home is her workplace. This is where she spends most of her time and energy, even if she works in the marketplace. This is where people will come in and comment on 'her' decorating... God tells the man (in the book of Genesis) that he is to be the provider, and He tells the woman (in the book of Titus) to be the keeper or guardian of the home. So even if she is working, as the Proverbs 31 woman worked, she still has the feeling that if all is not right at home, she is not right." – Chuck and Barb Snyder

B. Greek ergon means "work" and its "efforts." (Titus 2:5)

C. The Helper manages her _____.

"She also rises while it is yet night, and provides food for her household, and a portion for her maidservants." Proverbs 31:15

Discussion   *What three things would you want to do in your home right now?*

D. The Helper generates _____.

"She considers a field and buys it; from her profits she plants a vineyard." Proverbs 31:16

E. The Helper extends her hand to the _____.

"She extends her hand to the poor, yes, she reaches out her hands to the needy." Proverbs 31:20

"Therefore I desire that the younger widows marry, bear children, manage the house, give no opportunity to the adversary to speak reproachfully." 1 Timothy 5:14

Conclusion

Asking your husband, "What can I do to help?" can change your whole perspective about your role in marriage.

1. Do you feel the average husband feels that his wife actually puts him first in her life? What do you think would happen in marriages today if she did?

_____

_____

_____

2. What were your initial feelings when you discovered that the Lord instructs the wife to be the "worker of the home"? Explain.

_____

_____

_____

3. Think about how your mother fulfilled her role as Helper in her marriage. What did you learn from her? How did she shape your concept about what the wife should be in marriage?

_____

_____

_____

4. The vast majority of wives work outside the home in today's modern culture. How do you think this puts pressure on being the "worker in the home"? Many wives are starting to work "out of the home" rather than "away from the home" – what do you think about that trend?

_____

_____

_____

5. As you read through the verses in Proverbs about the virtuous wife – that she manages her servants, generates profit, and extends her hand to the poor – what thoughts are going through your mind? If you determined in your heart to fulfill such ideals, what would you need to change in your life and marriage?

_____

_____

_____

THE HEAD OF THE HOUSEHOLD
WEEK 2, DAY 1

Proverbs 31:27—

"She watches over the ways of her household,
and does not eat the bread of idleness."

Bob Ethridge, Sr., pulled Rick Winters aside after their Bible study. "Rick, how about going with me Saturday morning to the reservoir to haul in our share of bass?"

"I'd love to Bob, but you know how busy I've been with work lately. Saturday I've got to work half a day, and the other half I'm playing catch up at home with a 'to-do' list a mile long.

"By the way," Rick continued, "maybe this is a good time to ask you. How is it that you have time to do so many things, Bob? I mean, I know you're retired, but still – you and Alice always seem to have everything under control. No loose ends, no panics. Connie and I don't even have kids yet, and we can't seem to get everything done."

"Well," Bob smiled, throwing out some bait of his own, "come fishing with me Saturday and I'll tell you a secret Alice and I discovered that changed our marriage. It helps us get more done, and," he ended with an eye full of twinkle, "gave me more time for my bass conservation studies. Know what I mean?"

"Okay, I guess I'm hooked. But just for part of the afternoon."

Saturday, after getting settled in a "good spot" on the lake, Rick turned to Bob: "Okay professor, tell me this secret that's going to get Connie and me organized and put me on the lake four days a week."

"Well, it's actually just three days a week. Is that okay?"

"Very funny. To tell you the truth, once a month would be a start!"

WEEK 2, DAY 1

From the Word

What do you think Bob and Alice had discovered in their marriage? Perhaps your marriage could benefit from their Scriptural secret. It is illustrated best in the Book of Proverbs, chapter 31, verse 27, where evidence of God's plan for husbands and wives is found. The couple in Proverbs 31 ran their marriage on a plan. The husband tended to his civic and vocational duties in the community (see verse 23) while the wife watched over the ways of her household (and they were diverse!). The wife serving as a helper to her husband reflects God's blueprint for building an effective marriage – each spouse knowing and fulfilling his or her role.

For the Heart

Wife, how are you fulfilling the role of helper to your husband?

Are you comfortable with your role and responsibilities? On a piece of paper, make two columns: Clear and Confusing. Under each, list those areas of "helping" that you feel are clear between you and your husband, and those that could use some further discussion and definition. Show your lists to your husband and work together on your marriage's version of God's plan.

And husband – have you encouraged your wife "to be all that she can be" in light of Proverbs 31?

Husband: Head of the wife. Wife: Head of the household.

SCRIPTURAL HELPS FOR HELPERS
WEEK 2, DAY 2

2 Timothy 3:16—

"All Scripture is given by inspiration of God, and is profitable for doctrine, for reproof, for correction, for instruction in righteousness."

It was "Ladies Night Out" for the Ethridge clan. Grandmother Alice, her two daughters Betty and Lillith, daughter-in-law Deb, and Deb's thirteen-year-old daughter Kim were out on the town. Their monthly suppers together kept them in touch with each other and had been an Ethridge tradition for several years.

After gallant attempts to eat with chopsticks, they retreated to forks – and more focused conversation.

"Speaking of television, I saw an interesting thing the other day," Deb offered. "One of the daytime talk shows had a panel of women discussing whether wives should quit their jobs if their husband's job requires a move out of town. Or should the husband turn down his promotion or transfer, or whatever, and stay put so his wife could continue her career. Wow! – I was amazed at some of the answers!"

"Amazed at what, Deb?" Lillith asked. "That a wife's job could be just as important as the husband's? Or, heaven forbid, *more* important? A friend at the bank just went through that same thing, and gave up a very promising career to follow her husband across the country. I told her not to be afraid to suggest to her husband that he should give up his promotion so she could keep her job!"

"But Lillith," Betty responded, "that's so arbitrary. Marriage would be nothing but a series of negotiations and power plays if both the husband and wife are expecting the other to follow!"

"Where does the Bible say the wife has to quit her job?" Lillith asked.

WEEK 2, DAY 2

From the Word

Don't spend a long time looking for that verse! Scriptural guidance for specific personal situations – such as Lillith is asking for – is often difficult to find. Instead, consider 2 Timothy 3:16, which says that Scripture is profitable for instruction. That is, we know Scripture clearly says that the wife is to be the helper of the husband – not the other way around. In marriage, therefore, as in other leader/follower settings, when the leader moves, the helpers follow. Are there exceptions? Of course. A loving husband should take his wife's desires into serious consideration, and possibly even change his plans. But the *first* step is always, "Am I willing to follow the general Scriptural guidelines for my role in marriage?"

For the Heart

Can you think of a situation recently where you disagreed with your husband's plans for your marriage or family? Was your concern over immorality or illegality? Marital disagreements rarely are of that nature. They are usually about personal preferences or opinions, aren't they?

If necessary, perhaps you could talk with your husband about your disagreement, and reaffirm your desire to help him – even if you disagree, and even if he is wrong!

The first principles to obey are the ones we know today.

TWO FOR THE CALL OF ONE
WEEK 2, DAY 3

Ephesians 5:21—

"Submit to one another in the fear of God."

Bob," Alice called to her husband, "John called while you were out and asked if he could drop by for a few minutes tonight to talk. He said he had something important to discuss."

Bob stopped in the middle of the kitchen floor without putting the groceries down. *Pastor Lawrence? I wonder what he wants?* Bob thought to himself. "Okay – I'll be here. Guess I've been singing louder than I thought," Bob called to his wife.

"No comment," came the safe reply.

Later that evening, after cake and coffee, Pastor Lawrence loosened his tie and sat up on the edge of his chair. The time had come.

"Bob and Alice, after a lot of prayer and thought – and the counsel of your peers – I've come to ask Bob for his permission to be nominated to serve as chairman of our church's board for the next two-year term. I wanted to discuss this with both of you because you know that at our church this is a position of great responsibility. In the past, it has usually absorbed a large portion of the time of *both* husband and wife."

After another hour of discussion about the chairman's position, and their role as a couple, Bob and Alice promised to give the pastor a response within a week.

And until late that night, Bob thought prayerfully about Alice's comment when the pastor was there: "I guess this means I'd have to give up my ministry at the nursing home – if you take the position – right?" He knew she was right. The board's chairman position would certainly rearrange their lives.

WEEK 2, DAY 3

From the Word

In this situation, does the role of helper mean that Alice should do what Bob is asked to do? Ultimately, yes. But a godly husband will always want to make sure that he has sought God's will before making a decision. And Ephesians 5:21 gives good direction for this initial step. Perhaps Bob would suggest, "Alice, for starters, let's both release our desires – first to each other, then to the Lord. He will somehow tell us whether I should take this new ministry position – or not." Alice might reply: "Good idea. Ultimately, I want to do what God wants us to do. And I appreciate your being willing to give Him the opportunity to confirm this opportunity – or not."

For the Heart

In the wake of the modern women's movement, the above scenario may seem unlikely. How about to you as a wife? Does it seem outdated or unrealistic? Perhaps a fresh consideration today of your role as your husband's helper will give you a new perspective.

The next time you and your husband face a decision with opposite interests, consider this: If you sense that God is clearly calling your husband in a new direction, would He not also be calling your husband's helper as well (don't look now, but that's you!)?

God is efficient: His plan allows one call to serve for both.

ALL WOMEN ARE NOT WIVES
WEEK 2, DAY 4

Galatians 3:28—

"There is neither Jew nor Greek, there is neither slave nor free, there is neither male or female; for you are all one in Christ Jesus."

Focused on the sports page at breakfast, Bob was only slightly tuned in to the instructions David was laying out for his sister, Kim, that Monday morning:

"...and because I've got a big algebra test tomorrow I'd really appreciate it if you'd do my dishes after supper. And could you put a lunch together for me for tomorrow? Uh, ham sandwich – no mustard, please – dill pickle, chips, an apple, and... a surprise. Well, I need to get going."

"Whoa, whoa, Dave!" Bob interjected, looking like a traffic cop ready to stop a fleeing thief. Turning to Deb, who was poised with spatula in midair and a "who-invited-the-dictator-to-breakfast" look on her face, Bob asked, "What is this all about, Deb? Kim doing dishes and making lunch for David?"

A bewildered shrug of her shoulders was all Deb could muster, so Bob turned to his son, still standing tall and looking confident – like maybe eliminating the national debt before lunch wouldn't be that hard.

"David, what gives?" Bob asked, his rising impatience causing Bobby's confidence to dissipate. "Since when is your sister your servant?"

"Well, you know, Dad. Pastor Kallan said in church yesterday how God made the woman to be the helper of the man, and so it seems like it might be good for Kim and me to start practicing – I can learn to ask for help, and she can learn to give it! It makes perfect sense!"

David's confidence had returned. He knew this was a great idea.

WEEK 2, DAY 4

From the Word

David was a bit unclear on the concept, don't you think? Unfortunately, some husbands believe and practice David's version of the truth. To be a helper is not to be a slave. And to be a woman is not to be a helper to all men. When God created man and woman, He created them with equal standing in His sight, as Galatians 3:28 shows. Women were not created to serve men. Rather, wives were appointed to help their husbands. The difference is significant. In marriage, any husband who believes his wife is his servant has misread Scripture. And any man who believes women in general are to serve men has likewise erred – and will likely be promptly told!

For the Heart

Has your husband ever treated you more like a servant than he has honored you as a helper? What was your response? If you have stored up any anger or bitterness at all, will you confess it to the Lord today? God understands your feelings, but wants you to commit them to Him, lest they cause your marriage harm in the future.

Forgive your husband, and then plan a time to talk over this issue – with your pastor's help if necessary.

Men who seek a servant instead of a wife seek in vain.

HONOR WHERE IT'S DUE
WEEK 2, DAY 5

Proverbs 31:28b—

"...Her husband also praises her."

"As is usual each year," the president began his remarks, "the shift managers and section leaders from the whole plant voted for the Manager of the Year. And this year, Bob Ethridge, Jr. has won in a landslide!"

"Wow! What a surprise, Pete," Bob said, shaking hands with the president after making his way to the podium. "I had no idea!"

When the applause subsided, Bob looked at his plaque, his new gold watch, the audience – and found Deb's eyes. He took a deep breath. *Here goes, Lord.*

"Well, first of all, let's get one thing clear – I'm a manager, not an after-dinner speaker. So bear with me a moment," Bob laughed nervously. "I do appreciate this award, more than you know. But there's another person who should be up with me taking much of the credit. Let me explain," he said to the puzzled faces staring at him.

"Pete –" Bob continued, looking at the president, "and all of you – you need to know who makes it possible for me to show up on time, wear socks that match, eat a healthy lunch instead of a candy bar, and explains overtime to the kids when I'm not home on Saturday – and, well, you men know what I'm talking about.

"Since being promoted to shift supervisor two years ago, there's a lot more to think about. And to be honest, I'm able to keep a clear head and keep thoughts focused at work because I know that things at home are so well taken care of. And for that, you all need to thank my wife, Deb – sitting right over there."

WEEK 2, DAY 5

From the Word

"Wow! What a surprise," said the readers. "We had no idea there were men like that out there!"

Granted, it would take a noble and strong man to stand up in public and give praise to his wife. But Scripture records, in Proverbs 31:28, another husband who did so thousands of years ago. "Her children rise up and call her blessed," it says. "Her husband also…he praises her." What would make a man do such a thing? Probably, as in Proverbs 31, the absolute magnitude of his wife's "helpfulness" to him in life. Some things just have to be said! When a wife makes her husband's life a success through her stability, skill, and sensitive partnering – that is, her helpfulness – it is hard to keep it in. Be it ancient times or modern, the truth is hard to hide!

For the Heart

At the conclusion of another week examining your role as your husband's helper, let's take stock. Jot down two or three areas that come to mind in which you know you are significantly helping your husband. Thank God for those!

And would you consider this long-term prayer? Ask God to one day allow your husband to praise his helper in public – not for your credit alone, but for your personal confirmation that God has opened up new dimensions of success as you fulfill His role for your life.

Those who honor others will likely receive honor themselves.

Helper - Session 3

Introduction

What does God want to accomplish through your husband that requires your help and support of him?

Biblical Principles for the Helper (continued)

4. The Helper is to actively "manage the house" under her husband's authority as the

"_____ of the _____." (1 Timothy 5:14)

A. Greek *oikos* means the "home" and its "_____."

B. Greek *despot* means to "manage" and "_____." (1 Timothy 5:14)

"She opens her mouth with wisdom, and on her tongue is the law of kindness. She watches over the ways of her household, and does not eat the bread of idleness." Proverbs 31:26-27

C. Not passive nor independent, but _____. **(Proverbs 31:27)**

D. Not problem-dumping, but problem-_____. **(Proverbs 31:26)**

Discussion   *How do you feel about being the "Despot of the Oikos"?*

5. The Helper invests her life so her husband becomes "   _____."

"She makes tapestry for herself; her clothing is fine linen and purple. Her husband is known in the gates, when he sits among the elders of the land. She makes linen garments and sells them, and supplies sashes for the merchants." Proverbs 31:22-24

A. She earns her husband's _____ – "her husband safely trusts her." (Proverbs 31:11)

B. She contributes to his _____ – "she does him good and not evil." (Proverbs 31:12)

"The heart of her husband safely trusts her; so he will have no lack of gain. She does him good and not evil all the days of her life." Proverbs 31:11-12

"Her children rise up and call her blessed; her husband also, and he praises her: 'Many daughters have done well, but you excel them all.'" Proverbs 31:28-29

"Behind every great man there is a greater woman…and a surprised mother-in-law!"

 *Personal Progress in the Wife's Role as Helper*

PROGRESS POINTS			
	Progress needed	Progress acceptable	Progress great
1. The wife accepts God's call to be Helper.			
2. The wife prioritizes her energies to help her husband.			
3. The wife fulfills her divinely designated role as "worker of the home."			
4. The wife proactively manages the home.			
5. The wife invests her life to make her husband "known in the gates."			

3. One thing the wife could do right now in her role as Helper that would be a great deal to the husband would be _____.

Practical Points on the Role of the Helper

1. _____respect and admiration for your husband. (Ephesians 5:33)

Discussion   *What two or three things can a wife do to honor and respect her husband?*

A. Never _____ in public or tear down in private.

B. Always _____ in public and build up in private.

2. _____spiritually mature married women to encourage you regularly for support and accountability.

A. Who? _____

B. When? _____

C. Where? _____

D. How often? _____

3. _____your own spiritual growth and don't harbor resentment whether or not your husband is the spiritual leader that he should be.

4. _____ regularly that God called you to be the helper of your husband – and as you help, to "do it heartily, as to the Lord and not to men." (Colossians 3:23)

"About three hundred years ago a man lost his job in a customs house. He went home, broken-hearted, to tell his wife Sophia. To his astonishment she only beamed at him. 'Now you can write your book!' He answered, 'Yes and what will we live on while I'm writing?' Sophia quickly went to a drawer and took out a cache of money. 'I've always known that you are a man of genius,' she said. 'I knew that someday you would write an immortal masterpiece. So from every week of the money you have given me for housekeeping, I have saved something. Here is enough to last us one whole year.' That amazed husband went to his study and began writing. His name was Nathaniel Hawthorne. His book was The Scarlet Letter."

Personal Pledge

Get alone with your husband and review the following statements together. Discuss them briefly together. Explain your desire to move in the direction of becoming a loving Helper. Then speak your personal pledge out loud to each other.

Together   We affirm today that God designed the wife to be the Helper of the husband. We willingly choose to submit to God's design for our marriage.

Wife   I commit to you that I will respond to God's call on my life to be your Helper. I ask for your forgiveness for the times I have failed you and not been the Helper that the Lord expects me to be. I hereby pledged to be an active Helper who serves you with all of my abilities and with all of my heart.

Husband   I commit to you that I will respond to God's call on my life to honor you as my Helper. I ask for your forgiveness for the times I may have taken advantage of you as my wife or not expressed my sincere appreciation for how you manage our home. I hereby pledge to share my life more fully with you so that we can "run the race" as a wonderful team.

Single   I commit to honor and implement God's choice for the wife to be the helper of the husband. I yield myself to His perfect design for the role of the wife in marriage, and purpose today to prepare myself mentally, spiritually, emotionally, and practically to carry out His design in anticipation of my own future marriage.

Conclusion

Your support can mean the difference between success and failure for your husband.

Which would you say are the best ways to love your husband? What would your husband say?

	Husband's response	Wife's response
1. Arrange for the two of you to have a date?		
2. Take a quiet walk together?		
3. Help him plan a trip just for "the guys"?		
4. Buy him a gift of tools or clothes?		
5. Enjoy sports or recreation together?		
6. Share spiritual things?		
7. Work on special projects with him?		
8. Arrange a special outing with the kids?		
9. Tell him how much you love him?		
10. Sit down and really listen to him?		
11. Touch him, hold his hand, kiss him?		
12. Send him love notes and cards?		
13. Surprise him with something special?		

1. What were your initial feelings about the wife being the "despot" of the house? Explain.

_____

_____

_____

2. If you were to write a job description for the Biblical "despot," what three things would you include?

_____

_____

_____

3. What would your husband feel about this concept of you being the "despot"? What would he like? What would he not like? Do you plan on sharing any of these thoughts with him?

_____

_____

_____

4. Give a couple of examples of how you show your husband respect. When you find it difficult to "feel" respect and yet you choose to follow the Lord's command and show genuine respect – what exactly do you do?

_____

_____

_____

5. Do you think most Christian wives really focus their lives to make their husbands "known in the gates"? What do you think would happen in the heart of your husband if that was fully true about you?

_____

_____

_____

SERVING TO WIN
WEEK 3, DAY 1

Luke 12:34—

"For where your treasure is, there your heart will be also."

Janet and Sally sipped their iced tea as they looked over the lunch menu. Janet couldn't help feeling a little tense as she contemplated how to break the news to Sally.

"Well, I wonder how Sylvia's knee is feeling," Sally began, "you know it's only two weeks until tennis team begins practice again.

There it was. The subject Janet had dreaded – tennis team. "Oh, I talked to her yesterday, and she said it was just like new again!" Janet offered, putting off the inevitable for one more moment.

"Oh great! So I guess all the pairings will stay the same," Sally beamed, "looks like we're headed for another great season."

"Well, they won't be *exactly* the same," Janet began.

"What do you mean?" Sally wondered.

Oh boy. Here it comes. Janet couldn't put it off any longer. "I've decided to sit out this season," she finally uttered.

"What for?" Sally was as surprised as Janet had imagined. "What's going on?"

"I... I just want to take a break for a while," Janet explained rather weakly.

"Really?" pried Sally, "Don't take this wrong, but I thought you lived for tennis."

"Well, actually... that's why I'm taking a break," Janet replied, as she leaned forward in her seat. "Do you remember that Bible study we did on the role of the wife?" Sally nodded. "Well, lately I've been noticing how the times when Bill needs me most are in the evenings and on the weekends... basically the times when I'm gone to tennis practice or to play a match. I just think it would be a whole lot easier to be Bill's helper if I didn't have quite so many activities pulling me away from him."

Sally leaned forward, "Janet, I think that's great."

"Really?" Janet said, relieved. "I was afraid it might sound a little extreme."

"Of course not," Sally added, "What could be more important than your marriage?"

WEEK 3, DAY 1

From the Word

Jesus' teachings are full of valuable insights about life and relationships. One such example is His assessment of how the human heart works. Jesus said, "For where your treasure is, there your heart will be also." In other words, if you invest yourself in a certain activity, essentially you give away a portion of your heart to it. And over time, your heart "learns" to value whatever you choose to emphasize as your priorities.

Janet was wise to consider how much of her heart she should reserve for her first priority – her husband. That doesn't mean she should never play tennis again, or pursue other interests. It's just a healthy reminder that, at some point, the benefits of outside activities can stop being benefits. Especially when they prevent you from being the wife you truly want to be.

For the Heart

How about your schedule? Being the helper to your husband is not an easy responsibility to start with. But sometimes we wives can make it even more difficult on ourselves by allowing other things to crowd out our first priority. It's not that those things aren't important too. It's just that if you don't control them, then they have a way of controlling you.

As you read this, are there any examples from your own life that come to mind? Are there times when just "being there" would make your husband *feel* your help more? It may be as simple as switching around some of your errands to allow you to be "on call" during the times when your husband needs you most. The more "treasure" you reserve for your husband, the more your heart will gravitate toward him as well.

To improve your serve, make sure you focus on the right game.

HELPING FROM THE HEART
WEEK 3, DAY 2

Luke 10:41–42—

"And Jesus answered and said to her, 'Martha, Martha, you are worried and troubled about many things.
But one thing is needed, and Mary has chosen that good part, which will not be taken away from her.'"

Mother's Day lunch was winding down at the Baxter home. Ellen kicked her feet up on the ottoman to read the card Jerry had picked out one more time.

...But most of all, I treasure the time I spend with you!

Ellen looked around the room. Jerry was busy scraping the dishes and loading them into the dishwasher. The kids were gathering the scraps of torn wrapping paper into a large trash bag.

This Mother's Day felt especially satisfying to Ellen. She was finally in a groove as the lady of the house. For several months, she had been hitting on all cylinders. The laundry was processed like clockwork. She managed the shopping like a detailed inventory support system. She supervised the kids with astounding precision. Frankly, she was proud of her productivity and efficiency.

So when she read the card, she couldn't help wondering to herself, "Of all the work I do around this place, do they really treasure *time* with me the most?" The card was nice, but as she thought about that line, she couldn't help questioning the truth of it. Sure, it's what we expect a Mother's Day card to say. But do we really buy those trite sayings... *really?*

As she pondered, Ellen watched the others whip the kitchen into shape. She was impressed by their teamwork. Their proficiency was good, even by Ellen's standards. Jerry and the kids were in a world of their own. While Ellen had been the center of attention during their party, she was now virtually invisible as they focused on the jobs at hand.

Then it dawned on her. If she were to vanish from the scene, all those chores would still get done. In fact, they'd still do a pretty good job. Sure, she was unique in her ability to manage the household, but maybe the best thing she brought to the family really was just *her*... the time she spends with them!

From the Word

The story of Jesus' visit with Martha and Mary presents a contrast between two philosophies on serving. While Martha occupied herself with the *what* of entertaining, Mary was occupied with the *Who*. When Martha complained about Mary's lack of help, Jesus gently rebuked Martha for making more of a fuss over the food than she did over Him.

There's a great lesson for wives in this story. It's easy to measure our success based on our "To Do" list. But while cooking, cleaning, laundry, and shopping are important, we must never lose sight of our reason for doing those things. If we do, we serve the *list* instead of our husbands and children. Instead of God!

For the Heart

As the helper to your husband, a great question to keep in mind is: "Does my husband *feel* helped by what I'm doing?" Even though we're doing hard work, we can sometimes be guilty of serving ourselves with our chores. We receive satisfaction by completing certain jobs. We get peace of mind knowing we're caught up. And it's easy to justify our hard work in the name of wifely duty. Meanwhile our husbands may be longing to talk about a new idea, or just take a walk together and enjoy the evening air.

How's your radar working? Do you come up from the "engine room" once in a while to check where the ship's headed? Why not ask yourself this question: "Does my husband *feel* helped?" Better yet, why not look for an appropriate moment and ask *him*?

HOME SWEET HOME
WEEK 3, DAY 3

Keep the Head of your House at the head of your list!

Proverbs 31:27—

"She watches over the ways of her household, and does not eat the bread of idleness."

"Kathryn, a new deck would mean we could enjoy the back yard more," Scott pleaded as he waved the drawings in the air.

"I don't know, Scott," Kathryn hesitated, "a deck would be nice, it's just that I'm not sure I want one off the basement."

"Just think of all the extra room it would give us to entertain guests," he added. "But it's not near the kitchen... and besides, I'd just rather use the money to fix up a play area for the kids first," Kathryn explained.

Scott sighed one of those *I'm right, just trust me* sighs. This wasn't the first time they'd had conversations like this one. Scott was a real visionary when it came to the house. He had big dreams and strong opinions. Kathryn, on the other hand, was a little more laid-back. As a result, she usually ended up deferring to Scott whenever they disagreed on something about the house.

But this time, Kathryn had strong opinions too. After all, she spent more time at home than he did. She was the one that had to manage the kids in this space. Besides, she didn't *want* to entertain guests in the basement.

"Scott," she said in a final attempt to persuade him, "I just don't like the idea."

"Well, I'm not sure what to do then," Scott concluded. "I *am* the head of the family... so I guess I'll have to make the final decision."

WEEK 3, DAY 3

From the Word

So, who *should* have the final word? According to the Bible, the husband should defer to his wife in this matter. Scott is still the head of the family, but when it comes to matters of the house and its property, the Bible is clear. The *wife* is in charge of the home. When it comes to decorating, she should be given the final word. When it comes to remodeling, the plans should be drawn based on *her* vision of what the home should look like, if she prefers. According to Proverbs 31, the wife is free to manage the home, generate profit, and show compassion to the poor as she sees fit. In fact, Greek word literally describes her as the "absolute ruler" or "monarch" of the home. This is the strongest word in the Bible used to describe a leader.

Of course this doesn't mean the wife should be a tyrant about it. But it does mean that the wife's instincts should take precedence over the husband's when it comes to the home. And ideally, husband and wife will treat each other's opinions with love and respect.

For the Heart

This can be a touchy subject for some couples. It requires that the husband and wife be in complete agreement on this issue. The wife should not force the matter on her husband, but should be patient and sensitive to his point of view. Turning to the other extreme, it's not an excuse to dump an overwhelming number of responsibilities on the wife either. So it may take some time before couples fully understand and embrace God's design for the homemaker together.

What about your household? Are you reaping the benefits of having the wife manage matters of the house? Have you, as the wife, ever taken full responsibility for this part of your role? Is your husband on-board with this principle, or does he need some time? No doubt, it would be a good idea for the two of you to discuss it together.

It's not a woman's touch that makes the home, it's her two-handed grip!

THE REWARDS OF MARRIAGE
WEEK 3, DAY 4

Colossians 3:23-24—

"And whatever you do, do it heartily, as to the Lord and not to men, knowing that from the Lord you will receive the reward of the inheritance; for you serve the Lord Christ."

Patricia watched in amazement as her parents packed for the trip. She was looking forward to attending the family reunion together. And while she waited for her folks to pack their things, she reacquainted herself with the old homestead. This was the first time in two years she had visited her childhood home. She was taken by the way things had changed. But she was even more struck with how some things hadn't changed at all.

"Where in the world is my yellow shirt…" Patricia's dad bellowed from the top of the stairs. "Ruth, have you seen my yellow shirt?"

No, some things hadn't changed much. For the most part, her father was a sweet, gentle man. But his one pitfall was the way he fretted and fumed over little things. And whenever he did, Patricia's mom just smiled calmly and swung into action.

"I already packed it in your garment bag, dear," she answered.

"Mom, I love dad," Patricia began, "but I've gotta know: how do you put up with his unpredictable little outbursts? I mean doesn't it upset you that he takes your help for granted and always finds something to complain about?"

"Well, Patricia," her mother said softly, "Your father and I have regular heart-to-heart talks about that… and he's making great progress. But I learned a long time ago that trying to please your father can be a frustrating goal. So instead, I just concentrate on being pleasing to the Lord by seeking to please my husband. That way, we're both a lot happier. Besides, it's really God we serve anyway, not each other!"

From the Word

When the apostle Paul wrote his letter to the Colossians, he issued a powerful reminder for all Christians: our greatest reward is not in this life. Sure, our efforts may prove fulfilling at times. But often, they can be frustrating as well. And the longer we endure in this life, the more we tend to understand the fleeting nature of this world's riches. In stark contrast, God's rewards are not fleeting. Nor are they instantaneous. God calls us to a higher purpose; and He also calls us to a longer perspective.

For the Heart

How about you? Do you ever feel cheated? Does it feel like all work and no pay? Do you sometimes wonder if it's really all worth it? Would you find it more motivating if you could see some reward for your efforts? Then take heart! God sees everything we do. And when you serve Him, you can be sure that you will receive His rewards!

The question is: What would you do today as the wife if you knew you would be rewarded for it? Can you think of anything you did yesterday that you would do differently today? Is there something you would go back and change? God has settled the issue of our compensation. He guarantees our just reward. He's good for it, too. And that should free us up to serve our husbands with reckless abandon!

On earth, you're the wife of your husband.
In heaven, you're the bride of Christ!

TAKING AN EMOTIONAL INVENTORY
WEEK 3, DAY 5

Hebrews 12:15—

"Looking diligently lest anyone fall short of the grace of God;
lest any root of bitterness springing up cause trouble,
and by this many become defiled."

Something had been bothering Carol all week. But she couldn't really put her finger on it. That is, until Brian mentioned the Men's Weekend Work Camp at the church's Retreat Center. That's when everything started to come out in the open.

"But who's going to pick up your client at the airport?" Carol asked.

"David and Karl are meeting them on Monday instead," Brian explained. "So how long will you be gone?" Carol began to pry.

"From six o'clock Friday until 5 o'clock Saturday," answered Brian, "the itinerary's on the refrigerator."

"You know, Jeannie has her math test on Monday. She wanted you to help her prepare for it," Carol continued.

"I know, we went over the equations last night," Brian assured her, "She's got all the formulas memorized."

Carol felt awkward as she suddenly realized what their conversation sounded like. She obviously had reservations about something. After a long pause, Brian finally broke the ice. "Honey, is something bothering you?" he asked. "I mean, I'd like to have your support. But I'm getting the impression that you don't want me to go this weekend."

Brian was right. Carol didn't want him to go. But why? Certainly she wasn't against church activities. And Brian hadn't been out of the house for weeks. The Work Camp couldn't have come at a better time in their schedules. So what was the problem?

As she thought about it, her mind drifted back to a time more than five years ago... when their third child was just a few days old. Brian had been the head of the men's ministry back then. In a moment of unclear judgment, he agreed to drive the bus up to the Retreat Center for the Men's Weekend Work Camp, leaving Carol behind with their newborn at a time when she really needed him there. He had apologized many times over. She had tried to forgive him many times over. But somehow, she just couldn't seem to let it go.

From the Word

We've all had those days. Nothing is really going *wrong*, but somehow things just don't feel *right*. And before long, our actions begin to show it. In his letter to the Hebrews, Paul warned about the importance of guarding our hearts. And one important part of that is managing your emotions. Women tend to be more sensitive than men. So we're more likely to be affected emotionally by everyday events... and more vulnerable to the temptations that follow... like harboring bitterness.

For the Heart

A decorator takes notice of the strengths and weaknesses of different furnishings in a room before attempting to make everything work together. Similarly, you need to know what you're working with before you try to do the job of being the wife. One of the wife's most important resources is her emotional energy. So before you get to work, it would be wise to take an inventory of your emotions. You need to know how you are feeling and what your current strengths and weaknesses are.

On a piece of paper, make a column of words that describe the emotions you are feeling. Do you feel excited? Angry? Happy? Maybe some sadness too? List everything, even if some of the words appear to contradict each other. Then, beside each word, try to jot down the cause of that feeling. What triggered those emotions? Are there any feelings that need to be brought before God? Any that make you susceptible to weakness? Are you holding any grudges that would prevent you from helping your husband with *all* your heart? This simple exercise can help you face the day with peace of mind, and guard your heart against destructive emotions.

The mind is like a warehouse. Keep yours free of trash and debris!

Helper by design   *Genesis 2:18-22*

What kind of helper to the man did God design the woman to be? _____

_____

What does it mean for a wife to complement or complete her husband? _____

_____

In your marriage what are several ways that your personality, talents and skills complement or complete your husband? _____

_____

What does your husband most appreciate about you in your role as helper? _____

_____

In what specific way could you be a better helper to your husband? _____

_____

The help defined   *Proverbs 12:4*

Who defines whether the wife is helping in an excellent or shameful manner? _____

_____

What reasons to many wives give for determining in their own minds what kind of help their husbands need? _____

Describe a time in your marriage when you helped your husband based upon what you thought he needed, versus what he said he needed. _____

_____

In your marriage, how does your husband respond when you provide help he didn't request or want? _____

In what specific ways would your help be more valuable to your husband? _____

_____

A worthy helper   *Proverbs 31:10-11*

How does this husband feel toward his wife? _____

_____

What are several characteristics of the husband who is convinced his wife is on his team?

_____

Describe a challenging time in your marriage when your trust (the wife's trust) made all the difference. _____

In what areas of your marriage does your husband wish you would exhibit more complete trust in him? _____

How could you express your trust in your husband more adequately? _____

_____

The helper's attitude   Proverbs 31:12-13

What is true of the wise wife in these verses? _____

_____

What kind of impact does a wife's positive, willing attitude have on her husband?

_____

In your marriage, what task do you do most willingly, and which one do you fulfill somewhat grudgingly? _____

Why is it difficult in your marriage to exhibit a joyful and agreeable spirit toward your husband? _____

In what specific situations is your husband most frustrated by your resistance and apparent unwillingness to help? _____

Powerful help   2 Corinthians 1:8-12

How did the Corinthian Christians help Paul in his time of trouble? _____

_____

What benefits can a wife's prayers for her husband have in their marriage? _____

_____

In your marriage, what hinders you from praying more consistently and fervently for your husband? _____

_____

What are the three most important requests your husband would like you to pray for him?

_____

Will you make every effort to cooperate with God's plan ordaining the wife as the helper to the husband in your marriage? Affirm your commitment to God by initialing and dating this page.

_____
Your initials and date

Submitting-Session 4

Introduction– Understanding the word "submit"

How do you react when you hear the word "submit"?

Biblical Passages on Submitting to Your Husband

"Wives, submit to your own husbands, as is fitting in the Lord." Colossians 3:18

"Wives, submit to your own husbands, as to the Lord. For the husband is head of the wife, as also Christ is head of the church; and He is the Savior of the body. Therefore, just as the church is subject to Christ, so let the wives be to their own husbands in everything." Ephesians 5:22-24

"Nevertheless let each one of you in particular so love his own wife as himself, and let the wife see that she respects her husband." Ephesians 5:33

Biblical Perspectives on "Submitting"

Definition: "Submit" comes from the Greek word "Hupotasso."

1. "Tasso" means to _____.

2. "Helper" means _____.

Discussion   What area in your life do you find the most difficult to bring underneath the "Headship" of your husband?

1. Perspective #1: To _____ the authority. (Romans 13:1; James 4:7)

"Let every soul be subject to the governing authorities...." Romans 13:1

2. Perspective #2: To _____ the authority. (Hebrews 12:9; 1 Peter 5:5)

"Furthermore, we have had human fathers who corrected us, and we paid them respect. Shall we not much more readily be in subjection to the Father of spirits and live? Hebrews 12:9

"Likewise you younger people, submit yourselves to your elders...." 1 Peter 5:5a

3. Perspective #3: To _____ the authority. (Luke 10:17; Titus 2:9; 1 Peter 3:1)

"Then the seventy returned with joy, saying, 'Lord, even the demons are subject to us in Your name.'" Luke 10:17

"Exhort servants to be obedient...." Titus 2:9

Biblical Portrait of Submitting

*"As Helper, the wife voluntarily submits to her husband
by respectfully bringing all areas of her life under his headship."*

Biblical Principles of Submitting to Your Husband

1. Submit to your husband because God commands you to " _____."

  A. Present Tense – I am to submit _____.

Discussion   *What takes place in a man's life when he sees his wife
respectfully submitting to him?*

  B. Middle Voice – I am to submit voluntarily to my husband _____.

  C. Imperative Mood – I am to submit by my _____.

"Today I hear a lot about mutual submission in marriage. Mutual submission is like up-down, white-black, good-bad. It's simply impossible. If it's submission, it's not mutual. If it's mutual it's not submission.... Mutual means to 'share things equally' and submission means 'for one to be under the other.' Mutual submission communicates that marriage is a 50-50 deal where each partner isn't submission to the other. That is, the husband is to show himself to be under the wife and the wife is to show herself to be under the husband. All that sounds good in our world, but it is totally contrary to the Bible." –David Dewitt

Conclusion

When we take a step away from God's design for relationships, we take a step toward conflict.

1. In general, what is our culture's philosophy regarding the concept of submitting? Give examples of how this philosophy is demonstrated.

_____

_____

_____

2. What factors would you say have contributed to the misunderstanding of Biblical "submission"?

_____

_____

_____

3. Why do you think the concept of "mutual submission" is so appealing in our culture?

_____

_____

_____

4. Which aspects of your life are the easiest to "arrange under" your husband's leadership? Which are the most difficult?

_____

_____

_____

5. Can you recall a time when you purposely "submitted yourself" to your husband's leadership, even though it was very difficult? How did he respond?

_____

_____

TAKE A LOAD OFF
WEEK 4, DAY 1

Romans 13:1-2—

"Let every soul be subject to the governing authorities. For there is no authority except from God, and the authorities that exist are appointed by God. Therefore whoever resists the authority resists the ordinance of God, and those who resist will bring judgment on themselves."

Cindy hung up the phone and turned to her friend Mary. "Well, I'd better get going, Mary," Cindy said. "That was Bill, and he wants me to meet him at the attorney's office to sign those papers."

"You mean he's going through with that deal after all¿!" Mary was visibly shocked. "I thought you told him how you felt about it."

Cindy seemed unusually calm as she put on her jacket. "Of course I told him how I feel," Cindy explained, "and he still thinks it's a good idea."

"Oh no, Cindy," Mary exclaimed, "what are you going to do¿"

"I'm going to drive down to the attorney's office," Cindy said.

"But you can't actually sign... you know what an awful decision that is," Mary continued. Cindy just smiled. And that made Mary even more confused.

"How can you just smile about this¿" Mary asked.

"Mary, I've fulfilled my responsibility to tell Bill how I felt about it," Cindy went on. "Now I'm going to fulfill my responsibility to support him and do what he asked me to do."

"What about your responsibility to keep him from ruining your family¿" Mary shot back.

Cindy paused to choose her words carefully, "Well, I used to think that was my responsibility too. But Mary... you wouldn't believe the freedom I've known since I found out it wasn't."

WEEK 4, DAY 1

From the Word

Can someone really experience freedom in a situation like that? When you follow God's Word... absolutely! The job of the wife carries many responsibilities with it. But ironically, some of the greatest burdens we carry around are often concerns that God never intended for the wife to bear in the first place. Like the job of making sure your husband makes the right decisions.

The Bible gives very clear instructions for both the husband and the wife. The man is responsible for leadership of the family. The woman is responsible for following that leadership. Adding to God's instructions inevitably adds misery as well. But obeying His calling on our lives has a way of bringing peace and freedom, no matter what our circumstances may be. True freedom always comes from observing the principles of God's Word.

For the Heart

Have you ever felt burdened about responsibilities that belong to your husband? When he makes a decision you don't agree with, do you automatically think of ways to change his mind? Or do focus on your responsibility to get behind his decision in spite of your doubts?

This is not always easy for the wife to do. You may be forced to support a decision that will cost you personally. In that moment, you must remember that when you follow God's Word, you allow Him to have total control of your circumstances. This doesn't mean you shouldn't share your concerns with your husband; but ultimately, your only responsibility is to submit. Then, you can trust God to work everything out for the best!

Wait on the Lord, or put the weight on yourself!

TRUE, UNADULTERATED SUBMISSION
WEEK 4, DAY 2

Matthew 5:27-28—

> *"You have heard that it was said to those of old, 'You shall not commit adultery.' But I say to you that whoever looks at a woman to lust for her has already committed adultery with her in his heart."*

"What do you mean I need an attitude check?" Harriet exclaimed.

Cathy was a jovial person most of the time. But when she wanted to get her point across, she wasn't one to beat around the bush. And even though her friends knew this about her, it always caught them off guard when she finally spoke her mind.

"You're going along with Daryl," Cathy explained, "but you're not really behind him 100%."

Because of the way she lived out her strong convictions, everyone respected Cathy... especially Harriet. So she couldn't help taking her friend's accusation to heart. Cathy's husband Daryl was convinced that the time was right to sell their home in the suburbs and move into town. Cathy hated the idea. All she could think about was how much smaller the homes were there... and how she would miss their neighborhood. Cathy went along with Daryl's request to gather information about available homes, but she definitely had an attitude about it.

"Just look how small these bathrooms are!" she would say, "There are homes twice this big in our neighborhood for the same money!"

Cathy was going through the motions, but she was still arguing her case along the way. That is, until Harriet called her on it.

"If you're not going to support him, then say so," Harriet went on. "But don't kid yourself... what you're doing now doesn't count as submission."

Submitting-Daily Devotional

From the Word

One of the great recurring themes in the Bible is that God cares as much about our thoughts as He does our actions. Even if our behavior appears to be exemplary, our attitudes can still condemn us. Jesus made this point clear when He explained that, from God's perspective, adultery is committed at the point of contemplation, not the point of consummation.

This same principle applies wherever God's commands are concerned. When the wife is commanded to submit to her husband, it is not simply a matter of outward compliance. The wife is to yield at the level of her attitude as well. She still may not agree with his decision, but she must somehow find a way to take ownership of his desires and carry them out with the same intensity and passion she would her own.

For the Heart

Do you sometimes submit your actions to your husband while holding an attitude that is less than submission? When you do, in God's eyes you are just as guilty as the wife who openly defies her husband. This doesn't mean that you must mask your true feelings and pretend to agree with him. But given the fact that he is the head, you are called to make a deliberate decision to get behind him 100%. A true disciple of Jesus gladly gives himself to the cause of Christ — even though he may not understand it all. Likewise, a truly submissive wife gladly gives herself to the mission her husband declares — just because he is the head.

Are there any particular areas that come to mind as you read this? Any situations where you have submitted with your actions, but have protested a little in your heart? Have you muttered any cynical comments to yourself along the way? Go ahead and admit to yourself that you don't agree with him... say it out loud! Then resolve to support him anyway... with all your heart.

Don't let your husband have a mind of his own... join him!

GOD MOVES IN MYSTERIOUS WAYS
WEEK 4, DAY 3

Joshua 6:5

"Then it shall come to pass, when (the priests) make a long blast with the ram's horn, and when you hear the sound of the trumpet, that all the people shall shout with a great shout; then the wall of the city will fall down flat."

"That's the most ridiculous suggestion I've ever heard!" Stephanie blurted before she realized what she was saying.

Stephanie had come to Wanda because she knew her advice about marriage was always based on what the Bible says. But she had expected her to say something wise and practical... or at least something reasonable! So she was completely unprepared for what Wanda had to say.

"I mean... no offense," Stephanie stammered, "but give me one good reason why I should let him run all over me like that?"

Stephanie had revisited her circumstances a hundred times in her mind. She had an iron-clad case. Her husband was clearly in the wrong this time. And all she could think about was how to stand up for herself and put her husband in his place. So how could Wanda talk about "submitting" at a time like this?!

Finally Wanda was ready to speak again, "Look... I know it may not sound logical," she offered, still looking for the right words. "But a lot of what God does seems illogical at times. I mean, who in their right mind would try to take over a fortified city simply by blowing trumpets and shouting? Or why would anyone send a little boy with a slingshot out to fight a giant?"

Stephanie gazed out the window, her mind was beginning to make the connection. Could God actually be telling her to submit to her husband to test her faith... or perhaps to demonstrate some miracle in her life? There was only one way to find out.

Submitting–Daily Devotional

From the Word

It seems the most moving and memorable stories from the Bible are often the most outlandish ones. The waters part... the blind see... the dead rise. In each case, the odds are so tremendous that there could be no doubt that God's hand was at work.

Similarly, the concept of submitting to the husband can seem like an outlandish suggestion. At times it may feel like the most unnatural response you can imagine. We'd rather try something we understand... something explainable. But sometimes you must be willing to give up the explainable in order to experience the unexplainable... seeing God's hand at work in your life. Depending on your situation, submitting may seem like a downright outlandish suggestion. Why should a wife deliberately make herself vulnerable to her husband... especially when he hasn't proven himself trustworthy? We can all think of much more "practical" solutions to solve our problems and improve our marriages. But just as God's will is always perfect, so are His ways of bringing it about.

For the Heart

It's no wonder that submitting to the husband is not a popular concept today — especially when the husband doesn't deserve it. There's a tendency to say I will submit as soon as he _____... I'll follow if only he will _____. But conditional submission is no more acceptable from the wife than conditional love is acceptable from the husband.

How about you? Do you submit to your husband even when it doesn't make sense to you? Or do you only submit in the areas where he's proven trustworthy? Can you think of any areas where you might be holding back a little? Try something unexplainable today. It just might lead to some unexplainable results.

"It's a God thing... even we don't understand!"

A MATTER OF TRUST
WEEK 4, DAY 4

Matthew 14:28-29—

"And Peter answered Him and said, 'Lord, if it is You, command me to come to You on the water.' So He said, 'Come.' And when Peter had come down out of the boat, he walked on the water to go to Jesus."

Pastor Armstrong closed his Bible and looked up at the couple seated on the couch across from him. "So how would you say the story of Peter walking on the water applies to your marriage?" he asked. Jerry and Ellen Davis looked at each other as they prepared to give their responses. It had been two years since they first came to their pastor for counseling. During that time, their marriage had gone from near destruction to near perfection. Still, they were always eager to learn more. At their request, Dr. Armstrong agreed to meet with them for an annual "check-up" and to review what they had learned.

"At first," Ellen began, "every day was like walking on water."

"Explain what you mean," Pastor Armstrong said.

"Well, submitting to Jerry went against all my instincts. But I stepped out... and eventually, I discovered another force there to hold me up. It was like God's power was unlocked."

"And what was it like from your perspective, Jerry?" the pastor asked.

"When you submitted to me, that really woke up something inside me. It's sort of like I used to spend a lot of my energy defending my turf... subconsciously... justifying my right to be the head of our family. But ever since you did that women's Bible study on submitting, things have been completely different. Now I feel respected like never before."

Dr. Armstrong leaned back in his big leather chair and stared up at the ceiling as he pondered Jerry's statement. "So when you felt respected, why do you suppose that changed your attitude?" he asked.

WEEK 4, DAY 4

Jerry thought for a moment. "It's funny, along with that feeling of respect came a feeling of responsibility... a responsibility to love and to lead our family the way God says to. It's like when one person in a marriage fulfills their responsibilities, it has a way of calling the other to fulfill their responsibilities too. But it never would have happened if Ellen hadn't decided to trust God in such a radical way."

From the Word

No matter what God calls you to do in life — whether it's walking on water, or submitting to a man who may or may not be trustworthy — it ultimately comes down to trust... will you trust God enough to do things the way He says? When Peter stepped out of the boat, his decision wasn't based on the water's reputation for supporting a person's weight. He acted because Jesus had invited him to walk on the water. Likewise, the wife who submits doesn't base her decision on her husband's reputation. She submits because God instructs her to do so.

If there's one theme throughout the Bible that captures the essence of God and His love, it is the theme of distinction. Often, we use terms like sanctification, set apart, holy, and chosen... they all communicate the concept of distinction: God's ways are distinctly different from the world's. When such a foundational theme is worth repeating throughout Scripture, it's worth repeating in this series as well.

For the Heart

No doubt about it, submitting is distinctly different from our natural instincts, from the ways of the world, and even from "common sense." But when you factor in that God commands it, submission is the only choice that makes sense.

How about you? Have you reached the point where you're ready to step out of the boat and trust God in a radical way? Have you been holding back at all, because something didn't quite make sense? Sooner or later, following God comes down to will you trust Me? And if you want to bring your marriage to Jesus, you may have to walk on the water a little.

In marriage, as in life, the choice is yours:
you can walk on water, or skate on thin ice.

MAKE ROOM FOR DADDY
WEEK 4, DAY 5

Genesis 3:16—

"To the woman He said: 'I will greatly multiply your sorrow and your conception; in pain you shall bring forth children; your desire shall be for your husband, and he shall rule over you.'"

"Hi honey, how was your day," Jennifer asked as she gave Tim a welcome home hug.

"Great." he said, "but I sure am beat. What time do you want to have dinner?"

"In about half an hour," Jennifer answered.

Tim parked his briefcase beside the door and loosened his collar. He had just enough time before dinner to put the training wheels on the new bike in the trunk of his car. Tim couldn't wait to get it ready so they could all ride together after dinner.

"Oh, Tim," Jennifer said, "I promised Casey you would read her a story before dinner. She's been waiting in her room... would you mind?"

Suddenly Tim's whole emotion changed. He felt an unexplained frustration building inside him. His face began to turn red.

"Honey, is something wrong?" Jennifer asked.

"I don't know..." he stammered, "it's just that every time I try to plan something, you've already spoken for me... I just wish you'd give me a chance to initiate something with Casey once in a while."

Jennifer was startled. Surely, she didn't speak for him every time he tried to plan something... he must be over-exaggerating. Right?

From the Word

When Adam and Eve sinned, it changed everything about the way we live and interact. The curses pronounced by God in the Garden of Eden are still lived out in men and women today.

There is an important part of the curse God placed on woman that many seem to miss: "Your desire shall be for your husband and he shall rule over you." Some mistakenly think that the husband "ruling" over the wife is the result of her sin, but this cannot be — for two reasons. First, Eve was created to be the "helper" of Adam,

WEEK 4, DAY 5

which preceded the fall. As 1 Corinthians 11:8-9 reveals, the woman was to support and follow her husband. "For man is not from woman, but woman from man. Nor was man created for the woman, but woman for the man." Before the fall, God's design was for the woman to follow the leadership of her husband.

Second, how did Eve commit that original sin before offering the fruit to her husband? She rebelled against Adam's leadership and did not submit to him regarding the fruit. Genesis 2:16 teaches that God told Adam not to eat of the tree, and he must have then told his wife not to eat of the tree (see also Genesis 3:17). The path of authority went from God to Adam, and then from Adam to Eve. When Eve decided to eat off the tree, she disobeyed her husband and God.

The second half of the curse God placed on woman struck directly at the root of her own underlying sin: her rebellion against her husband's leadership. The curse made her decision to rebel even more painful. From now on, she was going to have to struggle against the original mandate of God. But instead of following and submitting to her husband easily and naturally, she was going to have to fight a new and unfortunate desire to be the leader of the relationship herself.

In modern terms, God said this to Eve: "Eve, because you rebelled against your husband, your heart is now cursed in this relationship. From now on, your desire is going to be to overcome his leadership and rule him — but, Adam 'shall rule over you.' Even though you want to rule him, he will still rule you because that's My will."

The curse of God on Eve wasn't to put her under her husband's authority – that was in place before the fall. Instead, the curse upon the woman would twist her call into something difficult, and at times frustrating.

From the Word

Occasionally, when two roads merge, there is a road sign saying *"leave gap."* This is a good image for wives to keep in mind. As you go through the day, are you consciously "leaving a gap" for your husband's leadership? Do you constantly reserve a way for him to change the course of your journey together?

As the wife, you can have incredible influence over how your husband leads by how you follow. Nothing will produce a great leader quicker than a great follower!

If you'd like to see your husband "in the driver's seat,"
first make sure it's not already taken!

Know the Lover of your soul.

What do you really want? Are you looking for an abundant life, real intimacy, and eternal purpose? Deep in your heart you crave these things, and deep in your heart is where God wants to meet you. Our devotional magazines will help you connect with Him and cultivate the only relationship that can give you lasting fulfillment. To find out more visit us at www.devotionals.org

devotionals.org

A RESOURCE OF
WALK THRU THE BIBLE
4201 NORTH PEACHTREE ROAD
ATLANTA, GEORGIA 30341
www.walkthru.org
ORDERS 800.361.6131
PH 770.458.9300

Walk Thru the Bible's global ministry partners with the local church by providing relationships and resources to influential disciple makers throughout the world. From the Amazon River to the plains of Kenya, Walk Thru the Bible is changing lives and creating disciples for Christ on a daily basis.

- Over **13.5 million people** impacted by live teaching in the past five years

- Over **60 thousand pastors and teachers** trained in the past five years

- On-the-ground presence in over **60 countries**

- Strategic **network of local leaders** worldwide

- Intentional **interdenominational** impact

WALK THRU THE BIBLE®

Global Ministry

*Partnering for lasting life change through transferable,
biblical teaching, training, and tools*

To be a part of this movement, visit **www.walkthru.org** and click on donate.

Submitting-Session 5

Introduction—Portrait of "Mutual Submission"

TYPES OF SUBMISSION IN EPHESIANS
1. Wives to Husbands (5:22-33)
2. Children to Parents (6:1-4)
3. Servants to Masters (6:5-9)

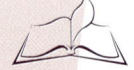

Biblical Passages on Submitting to Your Husband

"Submitting to one another in the fear of God." Ephesians 5:21

"Wives, submit to your own husbands, as to the Lord. For the husband is head of the wife, as also Christ is head of the church; and He is the Savior of the body." Ephesians 5:22-23

"Children, obey your parents in the Lord, for this is right. 'Honor your father and mother,' which is the first commandment with promise: 'that it may be well with you and you may live long on the earth.' And you, fathers, do not provoke your children to wrath, but bring them up in the training and admonition of the Lord." Ephesians 6:1-4

"Bondservants, be obedient to those who are your masters according to the flesh, with fear and trembling, in sincerity of heart, as to Christ; not with eyeservice, as men-pleasers, but as bondservants of Christ, doing the will of God from the heart, with good will doing service, as to the Lord, and not to men, knowing that whatever good anyone does, he will receive the same from the Lord, whether he is a slave or free. And you, masters, do the same things to them, giving up threatening, knowing that your own Master also is in heaven, and there is no partiality with Him." Ephesians 6:5-9

Biblical Principles of Submitting to Your Husband (continued)

1. Submit to your husband because God commands you to " _____."

   D. Biblical Context – I am to submit, not my _____. (Ephesians 5:18-6:9)

2. Submit to your husband "as to the _____" because it is "fitting in the _____." (Ephesians 5:22; Colossians 3:18)

"Wives, submit to your own husbands, as is fitting in the Lord." Colossians 3:18

"Wives, submit to your own husbands, as to the Lord." Ephesians 5:22

A. *Fitting in the Lord* describes the Christian wife's _____: (Col. 3:18)

Submit to the Lord's design of the Helper submitting to her husband.

Discussion   *How many times in the average week do you have trouble submitting to your husband? What is it about?*

B. *As to the Lord* describes the Christian wife's _____: (Eph. 5:22)

Submit to the Lord by submitting to your husband.

3. Submit to your husband "in _____." (Ephesians 5:23-24)

"Therefore, just as the church is subject to Christ, so let the wives be to their own husbands in everything."
   Ephesians 5:24

A. *Everything* means _____ even if he's disobedient or he's not a believer. (1 Peter 3:1-4)

B. Submission should include the sharing of your thoughts and _____.

C. Submission does not include the _____ – Don't break the law of the Lord.

D. Submission does not include the _____ – Don't break the law of the land.

Discussion   *How would your husband describe your attitude of submission towards him throughout your marriage? How has it changed over the years?*

E. Submission may include the heart-breaking but not the _____.

Conclusion

When you struggle to trust your husband, you can always trust your God.

1. Why do many women in our culture view submission as a loss of freedom?

_____

_____

_____

2. Name a situation in which it might be Biblical for a woman not to submit to her husband.

_____

_____

_____

3. Based on your upbringing, how would you say your mother did in submitting to her husband? How has that affected your attitude toward submission?

_____

_____

_____

4. Has there ever been a time when you faced a major "test of submission" with your husband? How did you do?

_____

_____

_____

5. What could you share with your husband today to let him know what you've thought about submission in the past and how you intend to approach it in the future?

_____

_____

_____

EVERYBODY OBEYS SOMEBODY
WEEK 5, DAY 1

Matthew 8:8–9

"The centurion... said, "... For I also am a man under authority, having soldiers under me. And I say to this one, 'Go,' and he goes; and to another, 'Come,' and he comes; into my servant, 'Do this,' and he does it."

The only thing rising faster than Lillith's blood pressure was the speedometer needle in her car.

"Where does Larry get off calling me like that?" she fumed. "He knew I needed him to take Allison today — but no, 'Something's come up.' Why I ever married someone who thinks it's his constitutional right to be in charge, I'll never know. At least I was in charge during our divorce!"

After the early-Sunday-morning call from Larry, Lillith calmed down enough to dress Allison and head for church. But as she mentally replayed his phone call, her high-octane anger turned her car into an invitation for a ticket. From out of nowhere, a policeman materialized in her mirror — another man just waiting to lord it over her.

Give me a break! Why isn't this guy in church or out catching dry dealers? she thought as she pulled to the side of the road.

She stood, sang, sat, prayed, greeted, and contributed her way through the first half of the service, oblivious to it all. It took her that long to process through both of her male-induced put-downs that morning. *Larry and a cop. Larry is like a cop. All men are like....*

"Turn with me to Matthew, chapter eight," intruded yet a third male — Pastor Dan Burton. "We'll continue our sermon series on husbands and wives this morning by looking at Jesus and a Roman centurion."

A Roman centurion, Lillith thought. *What's that got to do with marriage?*

WEEK 5, DAY 1

From the Word

Indeed! What does a Roman centurion have to do with marriage? In Matthew 8, when Christ meets this man, He is overwhelmed by the soldier's faith — and his understanding of a key principle in the kingdom of God: Authority. Like it or not, everyone is under someone's authority! Whether in the state, in the church, or in marriage, God has His authority structures.

Though Lillith had wrestled with submitting to her husband - and with authority figures in general — she was not the first to wrestle with this issue. God's ordered structures often run counter to cultural norms, but they are His way of blessing and protecting His people.

For the Heart

Regardless of your practice in submitting to your husband, you can probably identify with Lillith. All of us struggle with submission. It is against our human nature to "give in" to another.

Is there a particularly challenging area in which it is difficult to submit to your husband? As we begin this week of devotions on submission, would you pray for your ability to respond positively to God, to His Word, and to your spouse?

How to impress Jesus Christ: Live joyfully under authority.

WINNING WITHOUT A WORD
WEEK 5, DAY 2

1 Peter 3:1-4—

> *"Likewise you wives, be submissive to your own husbands, that even if some do not obey the Word, they, without a word, may be won by the conduct of their wives."*

Alice!" Bob, Sr., barked as he marched purposefully into the kitchen, interrupting Alice and Deb's conversation.

"I just looked at the mileage on your car. You were due for an oil change and lube 600 miles ago! I have asked you to please watch the mileage and let me know when it's due. That's what the little sticker on the windshield is for! Good grief, Alice, an oil change is a whole lot less expensive than a new car!"

Bob's back was all the reply Alice got as she tried to respond: "Bob, I'm sorry. You're right. I've been meaning to tell you…."

Deb wasn't sure what to say. She hadn't seen her father-in-law that angry very often. Alice looked genuinely hurt.

"I know how you must feel, Alice. I'd be hurt, too. You ought to go talk to him about treating you that way!"

Alice was quiet for a moment before replying. She knew she stood at a fork in the road. Down one way was the fleshly satisfaction of reprimanding Bob for the way he spoke to her, especially in front of Deb. And down the other lay the Biblical way, where she knew she would encounter the kingdom of God. She couldn't fail Deb, Bob, and God, by choosing amiss. "Yes, Deb, I think I am going to talk to Bob. I'm going to tell him, gently and quietly, that I'm sorry for not doing what he asked me to do. I believe I'll win my best friend back sooner that way."

"But, Alice…."

"No buts, Deb. God says a quiet spirit is needed at a time like this."

Submitting-Daily Devotional

From the Word

Was Alice right? When faced with a demonstration of carnality, is meekness God's will? Absolutely!

First Peter 3:1–4 is one of the clearest passages in Scripture on the "how" and "why" to respond to a husband's sin. And it is provided for wives. While Peter may have written this passage originally to address wives whose husbands had not yet become believers — and definitely were still living like it! — the principles apply to wives with believing husbands as well.

The "how" is to let the gentleness and quietness of your spirit totally surround your response. No preaching, no nagging, no retaliating.

Why? Because your life will be a living example of love, exactly what is needed by an inappropriate husband.

For the Heart

A frequent response of wives to Peter's exhortation is, "I've tried it. It doesn't work." That would be like a farmer saying, "I planted my seed this morning. Where's my corn?" Give God time! When you respond gently and quietly, trust God, because things are happening! Your husband is aware of his mistakes, and your love makes it more likely that he will change. Plan now to be gentle and quiet when the next storm comes ashore.

The mightiest song is often sung by the softest voice.

THAT WHICH IS FITTING
WEEK 5, DAY 3

Colossians 3:18—

"Wives, submit to your own husbands, as is fitting in the Lord."

The Thursday night Bible study at Betty's house had grown to almost a dozen energetic young women — all single.

After opening in prayer, and before she could even begin her lesson, a question was launched:

"Betty, I met Mr. Right today at work," Amy gushed. "No, I mean it," she continued, trying to talk over the group's ribbing. "I need to know tonight — what do I have to do to prepare to get married — next week? This is really it! I know it!"

Betty was trying to separate the wheat from the chaff in Amy's question. While this lively young lady could be the life of any party, Betty sensed a serious inquiry lurking beneath her lighthearted manner.

"Well, Amy, you never cease to keep us on our toes. Should we mark our calendars? Not yet? Good, because the answer to your question is going to take more than a week."

"And here it is: The best way for any woman to prepare to marry is to learn to submit herself to God. In good times, bad times, testing times, regular times — all the time. You must learn to submit to Him — and joyfully."

"That's it?" Amy asked. "I don't think I get the connection."

"Let me explain. Your chief responsibility in marriage is to submit to your husband, and to do it 'as is fitting in the Lord,' Scripture says. That means, you are to submit to your husband as an expression of your salvation and relationship to Christ. Therefore, the best way to learn to submit to your husband 'next week' is to submit to the Lord 'this week!'"

WEEK 5, DAY 3

From the Word

When Paul wrote to the Colossians, he was imparting a Christian "world view" that would shape all of their daily relationships. Christian people should give evidence of their faith. For a wife, the norm is to submit to her husband. Why? Because God's appointed leader in marriage is the husband, and to submit to the husband is for the wife a way of saying, "God, I honor You, and Your plan for marriage, by complying with it." In other words, wives should submit because it is fitting if they are "in the Lord," meaning if they are Christians. To submit to the husband is to demonstrate a spirit of submissiveness to the Lord. A lack of submission would show the opposite.

For the Heart

Are there not plenty of other ways that a wife can manifest the lordship of Christ in marriage? Certainly there are, but perhaps none so important as submitting to her husband.

Not only is submission the most important, it is also one of the hardest things for a wife to do — but, one of the most productive. Take a minute to sit down with your husband and ask, "Is there any way that my submissiveness to you, or the lack of it, lessens your respect for my Christian life?" If the answer is "Yes," hear out your husband, and take his comments to heart — and to the Lord, if needed.

How to "fit in" with the Lord? Submit to your husband!

WHAT JESUS DIDN'T DO
WEEK 5, DAY 4

1 Peter 2: 23—

> *"Who, when He was reviled, did not reviled and return;*
> *when He suffered, He did not threaten,*
> *but committed Himself to Him who judges righteously."*

"Hi, hon! Ooooh — I love it! You're fixing my favorite supper! Liver and onions — I could smell 'em in the driveway! Way to go, Deb! Deb? What's wrong? I know liver and onions isn't your favorite, but it's not that bad is it?" teased Bob, Jr.

"No, I'm sorry. I've just felt down all afternoon — discouraged, I guess."

"Why?"

"Well, you know the lady we met in Sunday School — the one that just moved here from up north? Beverly Landers?"

"I remember."

"Well, I dropped by her house this afternoon just to visit, and I learned more about her than we did Sunday. And some of it was pretty sad."

"Like what? She doesn't fix liver and onions for her husband?"

"Bob, this is serious. She probably would do that, or anything else he asked, if he would treat her better. I don't think he's a Christian — I wondered why she was in church alone — and apparently he treats her pretty badly at times."

"What do you mean?"

"Well, lots of verbal abuse, name calling — and I think when he drinks it gets pretty offensive at times. She was pretty careful about what she said, but I can tell it's serious. Her eyes welled up with tears while we talked. She said she didn't know what to do."

"So what did you tell her?"

Deb looked at Bob with her eyes brimming. "The same thing Pastor Kallan told me about how to respond to my mom's need to control. Follow Jesus' example, first and foremost, because God is a righteous judge."

From the Word

What Deb told Beverly Landers, and what Pastor Kallan had told her, is based on
1 Peter 2:21–23. It is unfortunate, but true, that some wives at times find themselves
in situations requiring their "non-retaliation." As Peter explains, when Christ was
reviled, hurt, and made to suffer by others, he did not return the words or actions to
His tormentors. Rather He "committed Himself to" (that is, submitted Himself to
the will of) God whom He knew would judge righteously one day. The temptation
for a wife to strike back, to lash out, and to seek revenge is great —- and
understandable. But, like Christ, wives must stay committed to their heavenly
Father who knows their condition and needs.

For the Heart

When was the last time you retaliated against your husband with an unkind word
or actions And how recently did you submit yourself to him — and to God — and
choose not to return the unkindness? Which of the two responses is most consistent
in your life?

  If it is the former, could you pause for a moment and yield your heart and will to
God? Why not pray, "Father, I commit myself to a non-retaliating relationship with
my husband. I want to be like Christ."

What one doesn't do is often as important as what one does.

WHAT DOES *EVERYTHING* MEAN?
WEEK 5, DAY 5

Ephesians 5:24—

> *"Therefore, just as the church is subject to Christ,*
> *so let the wives be to their own husbands in everything."*

Betty's best friend in the world, Sarah Randall, had stopped by to visit. No one could listen like Sarah, and when Betty's husband died, she and Betty spent long hours talking and praying together.

"So, what did you get Jack for his birthday, Sarah?" Betty asked over tea.

When Sarah's eyes fell, Betty's radar went off.

"Did something happen, Sarah?..."

"Well, I had this special fishing 'thing' — a rod and reel, whatever — picked out. Jack had it circled in a catalog. He really wanted it, and I'd been saving for it. But it was really expensive, and when it came time to order it I didn't have enough money to write a check. You know how tight things have been for us lately. And so I charged it on my credit card. I thought I could save the rest of the money before the bill came and get it paid off. No problem, right?

"But then, when Jack unwrapped it, and he knew how much it cost, the accountant in him started asking questions, and I finally had to tell him I had charged it. Since things have been so tight financially he had asked me not to use my credit card, and I had agreed. And we both had stopped using them.

"But then I just couldn't help it. I think I was more concerned about being embarrassed at not having a nice gift than I was about doing what he asked. Anyway, it sort of deflated the whole birthday thing. And, he sent it back."

"Makes for a bad party, huh?" Betty sympathized.

"Did it ever! I just didn't think it was so important. But I guess I was wrong."

WEEK 5, DAY 5

From the Word

Was Sarah wrong? What do you think? Her intent was noble — to do something nice for her husband. But her method was flawed. While the Bible does not say "do not use credit cards," it does say, "Wives submit to your husbands in *everything*." When the Apostle Paul penned those words (Ephesians 5:24), could he have meant everything?

The issue at stake is one of Biblical principles. Just as we are not free to pick one "small" Biblical command to violate, neither are we free to violate the instructions of one of His ordained authorities. It can make for more than just a "bad party."

For the Heart

As a tiny pebble in a shoe can make walking unbearable, so a small indiscretion against authority can take the joy out of that relationship.

Is there any small pebble of dishonor in your husband's shoe because of your lack of submission on some occasion? What would it take to remove it? Perhaps this week — even today — would be the perfect time to talk with him. Will you ask God's forgiveness, and then your husband's? He will walk with you easier if you do.

Submitting in everything means submitting in EVERY thing.

Submitting-Session 6

Introduction – Guarding Against The Attitude of False Submission

THE "SUBMISSION CONTINUUM"	
Which one of these are you?	
1. Revengeful	
2. Resentful	
3. Resigned	
4. Respectful	
5. Reactive	
6. Resistant	
7. Rebellious	

Biblical Principles of Submitting to Your Husband (continued)

4. Submit to your husband with attitudes and actions of genuine _____. (Ephesians 5:33)

   A. Respect means to show genuine regard and treat with _____.

   B. Respect must be shown regardless of your husband's conduct or _____.

Discussion   What would be the response of your husband if you showed him genuine respect, especially if he didn't earn it by his behavior?

"Wives, likewise, be submissive to your own husbands, that even if some do not obey the word, they, without a word, may be won by the conduct of their wives, when they observe your chaste conduct accompanied by fear. Do not let your adornment be merely outward — arranging the hair, wearing gold, or putting on fine apparel — rather let it be the hidden person of the heart, with the incorruptible beauty of a gentle and quiet spirit, to which is very precious in the sight of God." 1 Peter 3:1-4

5. Submit to your husband with a "gentle and _____." (1 Peter 3:1-4)

   A. Gentle means a heart that accepts God's dealings as _____. (Romans 8:28)

   B. Quiet means a heart of settled tranquility and deep _____.

 *Personal Progress in Submission*

PROGRESS POINTS			
	Progress needed	Progress acceptable	Progress great
1. The wife wholeheartedly/ consistently submits.			
2. The wife submits as to the Lord.			
3. The wife submits in everything.			
4. The wife submits with genuine respect.			
5. The wife submits with a gentle and quiet spirit.			

Discussion   Which of the five items on the chart is the most important to your husband Why?

The classified ad read: "For Sale: 1984 Mercedes, 240 SL. Loaded. First fifty dollars takes it."

Not believing his eyes, a man called the number to see if the "fifty dollars" was a misprint. A woman assured him it wasn't. She was indeed selling the car for fifty dollars, and there was absolutely nothing wrong with it. The man rushed over with his fifty dollars in cash, and as she handed him the title to the luxurious automobile he asked for the obvious question: 'Why are you selling a Mercedes for fifty dollars?' Well, my husband just phoned me from Las Vegas. He's there with his secretary, and he said he's leaving me. He went broke gambling and he asked me to sell the Mercedes and send him half of what I get for it.'"
   –"Dear Abby"

Practical Pointers on the Role of the Head

1. _____ anything you do that disappoints, frustrates, or angers your husband.

   A. I disappoint my husband when I _____.

   B. I frustrate my husband when I _____.

   C. I anger my husband when I _____.

2. _____ your husband for any past hurts blocking your submission.

   A. The area where I need to forgive my husband is _____.

   B. The most difficult area for me to submit it is _____.

3. _____ your submission so your husband feels respected.

If you wanted to demonstrate your submissive heart to your husband, which 3 actions would best communicate that to him? *(Choose three, then discuss together.)*

1. *Manage and clean the house?*
2. *Handle money and your budget?*
3. *Accept your overall leadership as head*
4. *Check before making any important commitments?*
5. *Help you with things that are important to you?*
6. *Show you respect in public and private?*
7. *Submit to you even when she strongly disagrees?*
8. *Not undermine you with the children?*
9. *Respond to you in your sexual life?*
10. *Share in the things that are fun to you?*
11. *Show you how much she appreciates and admires you?*
12. *Make you number one in her life?*
13. *Support you in your work and dreams?*

4. _____ upon the Holy Spirit to empower you to submit.

"He went a little farther and fell on His face, and prayed, saying, 'O My Father, if it is possible, let this cup pass from Me; nevertheless, not as I will, but as You will.'" Matthew 26:39

Personal Pledge

Get alone with your husband and review the following statements together. Discuss them briefly together. Explain your desire to move in the direction of becoming a submitting wife. Then speak your personal pledge to him out loud. If he feels comfortable, your husband may join you in the joint pledge and then speak the husband's pledge to you.

Together We affirm today that God has called the wife to submit voluntarily and continuously as the church submits to Christ.

Wife I commit to submit to you by arranging all parts of my life underneath you as head of our marriage. I pledge to submit to you "in everything" and "as unto the Lord." I commit to submit to you with a joyful attitude of genuine respect as my head even though I may not always agree with you. I will fulfill God's calling on my life by being your submissive Helper.

Husband I commit to becoming the kind of husband you find a pleasure and comfort to submit to as your head. You know how very important it is to me that you support and believe in me as your husband. I pledge to be sensitive to your needs and open to your wishes.

Single I recognize today that it is God's perfect design in marriage for the wife to submit to her husband as the church submits to her Lord, Jesus Christ. Desiring one day to have a marriage that honors and implements all of God's best, I commit to a gentle and quiet submissiveness being the standard for how a wife is to relate to her husband.

Conclusion

When you submit to your husband, you submit to God.

1. Is it possible to submit without an attitude of submission? Explain.

_____

_____

_____

2. Is it possible to submit without agreeing with your husband? Explain.

_____

_____

_____

3. When you fail to submit, are you more likely to be "resentful and resigned" or "reactive and resistant"? _____

_____

_____

_____

4. In what area is it easiest for you to trust God? Your husband?

_____

_____

_____

5. Name at least one way you could make your husband feel respected.

_____

_____

_____

HAND-ME-DOWNS
WEEK 6, DAY 1

Romans 8:9a—

"But you are not in the flesh but in the Spirit...."

It began as a simple exercise, but as Sandra listened to the results she could hardly believe her ears.

The women of her Sunday school class were asked to interview their husbands on an interesting topic: "In what ways do I act like my mother?"

The assignment called for the husbands to report on a wide variety of subjects including their wives' attitudes about work, household chores, parenting, romance, even cooking.

Each wife was to present the questionnaire to her husband and give him 24 hours to complete it. They would discuss their answers on the following Sunday.

Sandra's husband John was somewhat familiar with his mother-in-law, but since there were over a hundred miles between them, Sandra expected his responses to the questionnaire to be somewhat neutral. She was in for a surprise.

John not only had strong opinions on almost every topic, but he provided several examples from their marriage in the margins along the side of the page. He included descriptions of her mannerisms and several phrases that Sandra commonly repeats in various situations.

Sandra was speechless. But as she analyzed each response, she was unable to deny a single one. Those were her views about work. She did believe parenting should work that way. And come to think of it, she does say that whenever another motorist makes her upset.

She had never thought about it. She had certainly never planned for it. And judging by her reaction to the survey, she had never even realized it. But she had ended up doing things a lot like her mom. Good thing for Sandra and John that for the most part her mother was a godly, conscientious wife.

WEEK 6, DAY 1

From the word

Perhaps you've seen the bumper sticker that says, "It's official. I have become my mother!" While it strikes a humorous note, it also points to a real tendency. Our perceptions of marriage are strongly influenced by what our parents modeled out in front of us. The way you understand the role of wife is no exception. There's just one problem — your mother may or may not have followed a Biblical model on all points.

It could be that you have been given a great role model in your mother. But God's Word tells us that we should always look to our Heavenly Father's example first, an example that is described in detail in the Bible.

For the heart

People can react to their upbringing in a number of different ways. Some mimic the example they saw growing up. Others swing to opposite extreme, determined not to repeat their parents' mistakes. Neither of these approaches ensures a Biblical perspective.

Does your concept of "wife" bear the influence of your Heavenly Father? Or would you say it mostly reflects your earthly parents? Are there some areas that have yet to be brought through the refining fire of God's Word? Take a few moments to come before God on this issue. Ask Him to show you any areas of weakness. Claim your adoption as His child and commit to fulfill the legacy of His example.

Father knows best, but your Heavenly Father knows even better!

THE SOURCE OF LOVE
WEEK 6, DAY 2

1 John 4:19—

"We love Him because He first loved us."

Alicia found the pastor's question intriguing: "What's your L.Q.?" Alicia had never thought about her love quotient.

The concept of I.Q. was all too familiar to Alicia. She had heard it all her life. Class valedictorian, Phi Beta Kappa, Summa Cum Laude... and now a successful career in business.

Alicia seemed to excel naturally in school and in the workplace. It was almost effortless. But for some reason, the home front was a different story. Her marriage wasn't in trouble or anything. It's just that for all the work she put into it, the challenge only seemed to get bigger and bigger.

Being an intelligent lady, Alicia took her marriage vows to heart. She understood the emphasis on love. Over the years, she had read books and books about relationships and making marriage work. She knew in her heart that love was the whole key. But for the first time in her life, Alicia was facing a roadblock she couldn't solve. How does a person develop more love?

Whenever Alicia had needed more knowledge, or more information, or more experience, she simply went out and got it. She prided herself in her resourcefulness. But now she was embracing the fact that this issue of love was deeply mysterious ... somehow it was spiritual.

And when the pastor suggested that a wife could increase her love quotient — dramatically — Alicia was all ears.

WEEK 6, DAY 2

From the word

Have you ever thought about your "love quotient?" Your intelligence quotient pretty much stays the same throughout your life. But your love quotient has the potential to greatly increase. Imagine having a greater capacity to love people, even when it's difficult to love! The apostle John explained the secret of increasing your love quotient. Our love, he explains, is the natural response to the love we receive. To the degree that we have experienced love, we will give it.

For the heart

How about you? Is your love for your husband grounded on the ultimate Source of unconditional love: God? God has instructed you to be your husband's helper. That's not an easy task! Especially during those times when he might not seem so lovable. If you love using only your own resources, you'll run out too soon.

Has there ever been a time when you received God's love by inviting the Lord Jesus into your heart? If not, then you have no access to the real power of love He intended you to have. If you're not sure, take a moment right now to settle the matter. If you have already made that decision, are you truly tapping into that love on a daily basis through prayer, Bible study, and meditating on Scripture?

Take a moment to celebrate God's love for you and refresh your commitment to love the way you have been loved.

> *Hurt people hurt people.*
> *Loved people love people.*

A TIMELY CEASE-FIRE
WEEK 6, DAY 3

Proverbs 21:23—

> *"Whoever guards his mouth and tongue keeps his soul from troubles."*

Oops! That's the only word that could adequately describe how Hailey felt. She didn't mean to say what she had just said. It just sort of slipped out. And now Lewis stared off into his magazine while his face turned red with anger.

"I didn't mean it, honey," Hailey began. "Please, just let me explain."

It was too late. Hailey had said it. In time, neither she nor Lewis would even recall the exact words she said. Just that they were cutting, harsh, and bitter. And no matter how much she wished she could take it all back, she couldn't.

Hailey was under a lot of pressure lately. Her boss's demands were cruel and unrealistic, by anyone's standards. But with the new project nearing completion, Hailey felt she had no choice but to gut it out and give the clients what they wanted.

"Of course we can do that!" Hailey chimed into the phone. "I can have those for you first thing Monday," she promised. Lewis would give anything for some of the kindness Hailey was lavishing on her clients these days. He couldn't stand to see anyone treat his wife so thoughtlessly, stealing her happiness. And to top it off, now they were stealing the kind words that used to be for him.

When Hailey hung up the phone, Lewis made a suggestion about how to handle the situation. He was only trying to help. He knew it wasn't that great of a solution, but he was just hoping to say something encouraging, to spark an idea. Usually, he was her closest ally during such conflicts.

But this time, Hailey was flustered and deep in thought. Her anger toward her boss was building. She longed to tell him what she really thought… to give him some choice words. And it was in that moment that Lewis made his comments. And when he did, Hailey lashed out at him, instead. That's when she said it. And now she had to live with it.

WEEK 6, DAY 3

From the word

In military combat, the term "friendly fire" refers to casualties inflicted by one's fellow soldiers. In the heat of battle, it is sometimes very difficult to distinguish between allies and enemies. In a fast and furious attempt to eliminate the enemy who poses an urgent threat, comrades are accidentally destroyed instead.

The same is true in marriage. Every day, husband and wife step onto the battlefield together. When the intensity picks up, our minds often struggle to remember who the real enemy is. We can accidentally take out on our husbands anger and frustrations that were originally pointed at someone else. Before you know it, you can destroy your only allied support. God provides ample protection against such mistakes throughout Proverbs.

For the heart

Soldiers carry guns, grenades, and bayonets. Husbands and wives often cripple their relationships with nothing more than their tongues. It's no wonder James called the tongue "a fire, a world of iniquity. The tongue is so set among our members that it defiles the whole body, and sets on fire the course of nature; and it is set on fire by hell" (James 3:6).

Do you always speak to your husband with helpful words? If not, you might want to try this verse. Why not write it down on a piece of paper and carry it in your pocket? And when the urge to "vent" comes up, cease-fire for a moment and confirm your target. Guard your mouth and tongue. And ask God to help you respond lovingly. You'll not only win the battle, but over time you'll win the war.

Sticks and stones can break your bones, but words can destroy your marriage!

THE THINGS WE DO FOR LOVE
WEEK 6, DAY 4

2 Corinthians 12:10—

"For the sake of Christ, then, I am content with... hardships...." (RSV)

Mary was drawn to the marriage retreat by its juicy title: "Opposites Attract." Curt was simply looking forward to a weekend in the mountains away from work. But as the opening exercise got underway, both were suddenly uncomfortable with what they were hearing.

For the exercise, each person answered a brief survey to determine his or her own personality type. The test included likes/dislikes, attitudes, and temperament. Then each couple compared notes to see how equally matched they were. The point of the exercise was to discover if couples were identical, or if they were in fact more like opposites.

One by one the couples stood up. And little by little, the verdict came in. Not only were they not identical, but it almost every case it seemed that they were as different as night and day. How could it be? How could so many intelligent people suffer from poor judgment on such an important subject? Is it any wonder the divorce rate is so high?

Curt and Mary both thought about their own differences... how she liked organization, and he found it confining. How he enjoyed traveling, and she preferred to stay home whenever possible. The more they thought about it, the more they realized just how different they were.

As she looked around the room at all the mismatched couples, Mary couldn't help drawing the conclusion that marriages were somehow rigged — that people inevitably choose partners that bring out the worst in each other. But why?

Curt and Mary felt pretty good about how they had always worked out their differences in the past. But as they realized how many differences still remained, it was depressing. What caused this phenomenon? And what should they do about it?

WEEK 6, DAY 4

From the word

Often, the most satisfying things in life are the things that come with great difficulty. An academic degree, a business goal, an athletic pursuit, a sales quota. The harder we work for something, the more it seems to bring fulfillment. But sometimes in marriage it's hard to see the benefit — the purpose — of our difficulties. By working hard for something, we discover power and strength we otherwise would not have known. And as the apostle Paul pointed out in this passage, the ultimate discovery comes from finally tapping into God's power.

People wonder why marriage is sometimes so difficult. They have doubts, questions, and even remorse. They wonder if they married the right person after all. And they dream of reaching the point where things finally run smoother.

Often, the hardships we question in our marriage are specifically allowed by God for a purpose. While we dream of smooth sailing, God is faithfully going about the work of molding and shaping us. The very things we disdain can often be the instruments of our refining.

For the heart

Are their certain obstacles in your marriage — hardships — that you think hold the key to a better life? Do you ever think, "If only we could solve that problem kick that habit, change that attitude, *then* we could have the marriage God intended us to have." Maybe it's time to embrace those hardships instead, and thank God for them.

Remember, God is still in control. As you pursue His plan for your marriage, He will faithfully transform it — in *His* timing. In the meantime, there may be hardships. But be encouraged. When we are weak, He is strong.

When you just can't take it any more, He still can.

WHEN SUBMITTING IS HELPING
WEEK 6, DAY 5

Ephesians 4:16; 5:15–17; 5:21–22—

"The whole body, joined and knit together by what every joint supplies, according to the effective working by which every part does its share, causes growth of the body for the edifying of itself in love...."

"See then that you walk circumspectly, not as fools but as wise, redeeming the time, because the days are evil. Therefore do not be unwise, but understand what the will of the Lord is...."

"...submitting to one another in the fear of God. Wives, submit to your own husbands, as to the Lord."

Tracy and her mother, Vickie, had been going over final preparations for the big wedding. And since her mother had been successfully married for over 25 years, Tracy used the occasion to clear up this issue of submission once and for all. After Vickie thought she had explained everything, she discovered there was still more explaining to do.

"Okay, Mom… I guess I can live with the concept of submitting," Tracy declared to her mother. "Besides," she added, "Rob and I are so much alike, there won't be many occasions where I have to submit to him anyway."

Somehow Vickie sensed that Tracy still hadn't gotten the picture.

"What do you mean?" Vickie asked.

"Well," Tracy went on, "if Rob and I disagree on something, I can submit and trust that God will work everything out… even if Rob is wrong. But frankly, Mom, we never disagree anyway."

"Tracy… I don't think you understand." Vickie motioned for Tracy to sit down beside her. Then she began to explain, "Submission goes far beyond just yielding to Rob when you disagree. It's something you have to be proactive about… making sure at all times that each area of your life is under his authority... to maximize your potential together. It's one thing to submit whenever there's a conflict of interest, but that's such a passive approach to life... you could miss so much! True submission means you look for ways to make sure your life comes underneath him and supports his leadership. That's when your marriage really takes off!"

"So it's the same as being his helper?" Tracy chimed in.

"Well, sort of..." Vickie pondered. "It's a lot like your relationship with God. If your only interaction with God was to make sure you didn't violate His commandments, that wouldn't be much of a relationship, would it?" Tracy shook her head. Vickie went on, "Instead, you search diligently to know God's will... because the more you walk in it, the more you enjoy it. So you see, submission should help enhance your relationship with Rob, not just resolve your disagreements."

From the Word

With all the criticism submission gets in our culture, it's easy to think of submission only in the context of a confrontation. But God did not create the concept of submission simply for the purpose of resolving power struggles. He intended it to help couples accomplish more of what He has planned for them. As the wife is the helper to the husband, submission is the ultimate expression of help. An attitude of submission says to the man, "I am fully devoted to my God-given task of helping."

This series divides the role of the wife into Helping and Submitting. But in reality, the two go hand in hand. The wife who is truly helpful has an attitude of submission. And the wife who is truly submissive has an attitude of helpfulness. The key to both lies in being surrendered to the Holy Spirit.

For the Heart

So, what is your view on submission? Is it a concept you call upon whenever you and your husband don't see eye to eye? Or is it something you're proactive about? Do you search diligently for opportunities to submit? Bringing your life under your husband's leadership (submission) has the same effect as getting behind him (helping) and giving him your support. The net result is that when you submit, you enable yourself and your husband to blossom together in God's will.

Get underneath your husband's authority and you both come out on top!

Submitting–Session 6

Submission's Extent Ephesians 5:22-24

To what extent are wives to submit to their own husbands? _____

_____

As you think of the typical marriage, what percentage of the time does the wife submit to her husband? _____

_____

In your marriage, what hinders you from submitting to your husband "in everything"?

_____

In what specific area of your marriage would your submission mean the most to your husband? _____

_____

Submission's School Hebrews 5:5-8

What impact did suffering have on Christ's obedience? _____

_____

What are some of the emotions you might experience in the process of learning obedience as it relates to submission? _____

_____

From your marriage, give an example of a time when you obeyed your husband, even though it was extremely difficult._____

_____

How have you learned obedience so far in your marriage? _____

_____

Submission's Power 1 Peter 5:5-7

What character quality is closely associated with submission in this passage?_____

_____

How does a humble person speak and act? _____

_____

In what areas of your marriage do you struggle with pride, or the need to prove you are right?

_____

How have you experienced God's grace when you humbled yourself in your marriage?

_____

_____

In what aspect of your marriage would a humble spirit have the greatest impact? _____

_____

Submission's Conduct   1 Peter 3:1-6

How is a wife to show submission to the husband?_____

_____

Describe the conduct of a godly wife._____

_____

In your marriage, what aspects of your behavior are the most winsome and attractive to
your husband?_____

_____

At this time, in what area of your marriage should you trust God rather than attempt to ver-
bally influence your husband? _____

_____

Submission's Honor   Ephesians 5:33

What key word in this passage summarizes how a wife is to relate to her husband?_____

_____

How does a husband when his wife expresses her honor and respect for him? _____

_____

In your marriage, what do you respect the most about your husband?_____

_____

In what aspect of your marriage would your demonstration of respect for your husband
make the greatest difference to him? _____

_____

Will you commit yourself to honor and elevate your responsibility to submit to your husband in marriage?
Affirm your commitment by initialing and dating this page.

_____
Your initials and date

Transformers:

With Scripture on one side and a prayer on the other, these cards will help provide the daily discipline you need to stay committed to your wife and marriage. Each of the six video sessions comes with two cards, one for morning and one for the evening.

Use the same two session cards every day for a week, and be sure to check off the days of the week in the boxes provided. Before long, you'll feel those verses sinking deep into your soul. And transforming all that you are.

SESSION 1
The Morning Transformer

TRANSFORMATION THRU RENEWING THE MIND

"And the LORD God said, 'It is not good that man should be alone; I will make him a helper comparable to him.'" – **Genesis 2:18**

"For man is not from woman, but woman from man. Nor was man created for the woman, but woman for the man." – **1 Corinthians 11:8-9**

"Fear not, for I am with you; be not dismayed, for I am your God. I will strengthen you, yes, I will help you, I will uphold you with My righteous right hand." – **Isaiah 41:10**

Su	M	Tu	W	Th	F	Sa

SESSION 1
The Evening Transformer

TRANSFORMATION THRU RENEWING THE MIND

"...male and female He created them. Then God blessed them...." – **Genesis 1:27-28**

"He who finds a wife finds a good thing, and obtains favor from the LORD." – **Proverbs 18:22**

"An excellent wife is the crown of her husband...." – **Proverbs 12:4**

"Behold, God is my helper; the Lord is with those who uphold my life." – **Psalm 54:4**

Su	M	Tu	W	Th	F	Sa

SESSION 2
The Morning Transformer

TRANSFORMATION THRU RENEWING THE MIND

"That they admonish the young women to love their husbands, to love their children, to be discreet, chaste, homemakers, good, obedient to their own husbands, that the word of God may not be blasphemed." – **Titus 2:4-5**

"She also rises while it is yet night, and provides food for her household, and a portion for her maidservants. She considers a field and buys it; from her profits she plants a vineyard." – **Proverbs 31:15-16**

Su	M	Tu	W	Th	F	Sa

Dear Lord,

As I face another day, I also face the reality that I desperately need Your help if I am to do all that You have called me to do today. I confess that if I truly adopt Your perspective on the role of the wife, at times I can feel overwhelmed. It's hard to think of myself as my husband's helper when so often I am the one who needs help. Who will help me, Lord?

Thanks be to Your Name. You are my Helper! You have given me life! You have given me a husband to share it with! And You have given us both a mission to accomplish together. Thank You for making it so clear what roles we are to play as we work together to bring You glory. Help me now to be the helper You have called me to be. Make me sensitive to the different ways that I can be a help to my husband. Enable me to anticipate his needs. And show me how to come alongside him to help him become everything he can be in You. In Jesus' name I pray, amen.

Su · M · Tu · W · Th · F · Sa

Dear God,

What an honor and a privilege it is to come into Your presence today. You are holy... the God of the universe, and it is Your desire for me to come before You! I am the object of Your love and the recipient of Your grace and favor!

You esteem me highly, and have appointed me to the highest of all callings — to be one of Your helpers, Lord. I confess that I have not always understood this calling. I have often viewed it as a subordinate role. But how could it be, when it is the role You have chosen for Yourself? When I act as my husband's helper, I identify myself with You!

Thank You for putting such a high value on both me and my husband. Help me today to walk in Your will by fulfilling my role as his wife. Help me to be a "good thing," his crown, and his helper. In Jesus' name I pray, amen.

Su · M · Tu · W · Th · F · Sa

Dear Heavenly Father,

I come before You this morning in recognition that You are the Creator of all things. You alone have created man and woman. You have ordained marriage and designed the way man and woman should function together.

Lord, the world around me rages against Your will for me. The role of the wife is often distorted and confused. And I confess that I have not always held to your calling for me in marriage. I have not always been my husband's helper. I have failed to assist, encourage, and support him.

I turn to You now, Lord, and embrace Your will for me. Thank you for assigning me to the highest calling of all — to be the helper. And thank You especially for modeling that calling for me through the person of Jesus Christ and the ministry of the Holy Spirit. Help me today to reflect the incredible work You have performed in me through my salvation, and are continuing to do in me as You conform me into the image of Your Son, in Whose name I pray, amen.

Su · M · Tu · W · Th · F · Sa

SESSION 2
The Evening Transformer

TRANSFORMATION THRU RENEWING THE MIND

"Therefore I desire that the younger widows marry, bear children, manage the house, give no opportunity to the adversary to speak reproachfully."
– 1 Timothy 5:14

"Her lamp does not go out by night. She stretches out her hands to the distaff, and her hand holds the spindle. She extends her hand to the poor, yes, she reaches out her hands to the needy. She is not afraid of snow for her household, for all her household is clothed with scarlet.... She watches over the ways of her household, and does not eat the bread of idleness." **– Proverbs 31: 18b-21, 27**

SESSION 3
The Morning Transformer

TRANSFORMATION THRU RENEWING THE MIND

"The heart of her husband safely trusts her; so he will have no lack of gain. She does him good and not evil all the days of her life."
– Proverbs 31:11-12

"She makes tapestry for herself; her clothing is fine linen and purple. Her husband is known in the gates, when he sits among the elders of the land. She makes linen garments and sells them, and supplies sashes for the merchants."
– Proverbs 31:22-24

SESSION 3
The Evening Transformer

TRANSFORMATION THRU RENEWING THE MIND

"She opens her mouth with wisdom, and on her tongue is the law of kindness. She watches over the ways of her household, and does not eat the bread of idleness. Her children rise up and call her blessed; her husband also, and he praises her: 'Many daughters have done well, but you excel them all.'"
– Proverbs 31:26-29

"Let all those rejoice who put their trust in You; let them ever shout for joy, because You defend them; let those also who love Your name be joyful in You. For You, O Lord, will bless the righteous; with favor You will surround him as with a shield."
– Psalm 5:11-12

SESSION 3
The Evening Transformer
TRANSFORMATION THRU RENEWING THE MIND

Lord of the day and night,

I come to you at the conclusion of this day, thanking You that this is the day You have made! You created this day and placed me in it for a purpose.

Father, I ask that You would renew my heart. Refresh my conviction to be my husband's helper. Help me to focus on this calling, giving it the same priority in my life that You do.

Awesome God, thank You that I have not walked through this day alone. You are always ahead of me, preparing the way. You walk beside me, giving me strength. And You come along behind me, ensuring my success. Help me to finish this day strong, and to fulfill my mission to help my husband. I pray this in the name of Jesus Christ, amen.

SESSION 3
The Morning Transformer
TRANSFORMATION THRU RENEWING THE MIND

Good Morning Lord!

Lord, as I awaken to this day, awaken me to the opportunity that lies before me. Help me to see this day as a new chance to be the helper to my husband.

Father, I confess that my natural instinct is to think of ways to help myself. When I wake up in the morning, my first thoughts are usually about what the day holds in store for ME. Lord, I know that You provide for all my needs. You have made it possible for me to focus on helping others. And You have called me to be the helper of my husband.

Lord, help me to wake up in the morning thinking about my husband's needs. Let my first inclination be to come alongside him and help him become all that you have created him to be. By Your power, I can do this today. I praise You, and thank You in Jesus' name, amen.

SESSION 2
The Evening Transformer
TRANSFORMATION THRU RENEWING THE MIND

Dear Heavenly Father,

You are a God of order and amazing creativity! All around me are examples of Your power to create and rule! You manage the universe with majesty and perfection. What an honor it is that have you have given me a portion of your world to manage. And yet, it is not mine, but Yours — I am a steward entrusted by You to perform the work of ruling my house.

Lord, help me to manage this portion of Your kingdom well! Father, help me to examine my personality, my talents, and my strengths to determine the best management strategy for me. You have created me, God, and You understand my situation better that I do. Show me how to apply myself today so that I can faithfully steward this house in a way that pleases You! I ask this in Jesus' name, amen.

"Wives, submit to your own husbands, as is fitting in the Lord." – **Colossians 3:18**

"Wives, submit to your own husbands, as to the Lord. For the husband is head of the wife, as also Christ is head of the church; and He is the Savior of the body. Therefore, just as the church is subject to Christ, so let the wives be to their own husbands in everything. – **Ephesians 5:22-24**

"Nevertheless let each one of you in particular so love his own wife as himself, and let the wife see that she respects her husband." – **Ephesians 5:33**

"Let every soul be subject to the governing authorities. For there is no authority except from God, and the authorities that exist are appointed by God. Therefore whoever resists the authority resists the ordinance of God, and those who resist will bring judgment on themselves. For rulers are not a terror to good works, but to evil. Do you want to be unafraid of the authority? Do what is good, and you will have praise from the same." – **Romans 13:1-3**

"Do not let your good be spoken of as evil; for the kingdom of God... is righteousness and peace and joy in the Holy Spirit. For he who serves Christ in these things is acceptable to God and approved by men. Therefore let us pursue the things which make for peace and the things by which one may edify another." – **Romans 14:16-19**

"Therefore submit yourselves to every ordinance of man for the Lord's sake, whether to the king as supreme, or to governors, as to those who are sent by him for the punishment of evildoers and for the praise of those who do good. For this is the will of God, that by doing good you may put to silence the ignorance of foolish men—as free, yet not using liberty as a cloak for vice, but as bondservants of God. Honor all people. Love the brotherhood. Fear God. Honor the king." – **1 Peter 2:13-17**

The Morning Transformer

TRANSFORMATION THRU RENEWING THE MIND

Everlasting Father,

The sun has risen right on schedule again! All creation calls attention to Your power and dominion. You have created the world and ordered its contents. You have determined the path of the earth, the moon, and the sun! You have determined my path as well.

I acknowledge Your lordship over the universe, and over me. You have set the world in order, and established all authority. By serving Your ordained authorities, I serve You! Lord, I longed to bring honor to Your name. Thank You for giving me the privilege of honoring You as I submit to my husband's authority. Father, please guide him and direct his decisions, attitudes, and desires to help us both accomplish Your will through our marriage. Thank You that we, together, are Your creation and vital participants in Your kingdom. Praise be to God! Amen!

The Evening Transformer

TRANSFORMATION THRU RENEWING THE MIND

Giving God,

Thank You for modeling the attitude of submission for me in the person of Jesus Christ. I marvel at how He surrendered His will, choosing instead to fulfill the greater purposes of Your kingdom.

Lord, I am inspired by Your example! I commit to You the rest of this day that You have given me. I lay it down before You. As an act of submission to You, I commit now to submit to my husband with all my heart throughout the remainder of this day. Lord, grant me the righteousness and peace and joy that Your Word offers. Open my eyes, I pray, and let me see the big picture... the greater purposes that You seek to accomplish with the help of my submissive heart. Thank You for allowing me this opportunity to fulfill the greater purposes of Your kingdom, just as Jesus did when He submitted daily. Thank You for giving my life such profound purpose. In Jesus' name I pray, amen.

The Morning Transformer

TRANSFORMATION THRU RENEWING THE MIND

Heavenly Father,

It is not my natural instinct to submit to authority. I confess that even when I do submit, it is often when it is convenient and does not cost me personally. But Lord, when it comes to sacrificing my independence, and yielding instead to my husband's leadership, I struggle to be fully obedient. Yes, my actions can be described as obedient... but I have not made it the first desire of my heart to seek out ways to submit myself to him. I do not always search diligently for opportunities to bring an area of my life under his authority. I have been passive, rather than proactive, with Your command to submit. I confess this, Lord. Cleanse me, I pray! Give me the will to lay down my will. Help me to submit in a manner that pleases You. I pray this in the name of Jesus Christ, amen.

The Evening Transformer

TRANSFORMATION THRU RENEWING THE MIND

"Wives, submit to your own husbands, as to the Lord. For the husband is head of the wife, as also Christ is head of the church; and He is the Savior of the body. Therefore, just as the church is subject to Christ, so let the wives be to their own husbands in everything." – **Ephesians 5:24**

"Therefore humble yourselves under the mighty hand of God, that He may exalt you in due time, casting all your care upon Him, for He cares for you." – **1 Peter 5:6-7**

Su M Tu W Th F Sa

The Morning Transformer

TRANSFORMATION THRU RENEWING THE MIND

"Wives, likewise, be submissive to your own husbands, that even if some do not obey the word, they, without a word, may be won by the conduct of their wives, when they observe your chaste conduct accompanied by fear. Do not let your adornment be merely outward— arranging the hair, wearing gold, or putting on fine apparel— rather let it be the hidden person of the heart, with the incorruptible beauty of a gentle and quiet spirit, to which is very precious in the sight of God." – **1 Peter 3:1-4**

Su M Tu W Th F Sa

The Evening Transformer

TRANSFORMATION THRU RENEWING THE MIND

"He went a little farther and fell on His face, and prayed, saying, 'O My Father, if it is possible, let this cup pass from Me; nevertheless, not as I will, but as You will.'" – **Matthew 26:39**

"...being confident of this very thing, that He who has begun a good work in you will complete it until the day of Jesus Christ." – **Philippians 1:6**

"I will worship toward Your holy temple, and praise Your name. For Your lovingkindness and Your truth; for You have magnified Your word above all Your name. In the day when I cried out, You answered me, and made me bold with strength in my soul. The Lord will perfect that which concerns me; your mercy, O Lord, endures forever; do not forsake the works of your hands." – **Psalm 138:2-3; 8**

Su M Tu W Th F Sa

The Evening Transformer

Lord of Love,

Thank You again for the example of submission You have given me in the person of Jesus Christ. Thank You that He made Your will His first priority and His relentless pursuit. Just as He prayed, seeking Your will in each moment, I also renew myself to Your will for my life right now.

Father, I know that I am not yet fully conformed to Christ in all my life. I know that You long to refine me even further. As I reflect on this day, I also pause in the middle of this process You have begun in me — molding me into the image of Christ. As my husband's wife, I see that submission is an area of utmost importance to You. Speak to my heart right now, I pray. Show me how You would have me fulfill Your calling on our marriage. Give me boldness and strength, Father, to live the remainder of our days together so that our marriage can bring glory and honor to Your holy name! This is my prayer, in the name of Jesus Christ, amen!

Su M Tu W Th F Sa

The Morning Transformer

Dear Heavenly Father,

Thank You for keeping me safe through the night. Thank You for waking me to a new day. And most of all, thank You for waking me spiritually to a new opportunity to live this day in a way that pleases You.

I have been asleep, Lord...asleep to the importance of keeping an attitude of submission. There have been times when I have submitted outwardly, but inwardly I have been resentful and rebellious. I have allowed submission to be a matter of convenience for me, rather than my first pursuit. Thank You for teaching me to approach submission from the perspective of my attitude first.

Father, cleanse me of my sin. Create in me a clean heart right now. Put in me an attitude of submission. And help me to make my submission not merely outward, but let it emanate from the hidden person of the heart. I ask this in the name of Jesus Christ, amen.

Su M Tu W Th F Sa

The Evening Transformer

Dear Lord,

I pause now to renew my mind to Your will. How easily I become engrossed in my daily activities. How quickly I lose sight of the simple priorities that You have set before me. How often I fail to recall the sacrificial love of Jesus Christ and the example of submission He lived out for me.

I pray that this day would be a day about which You can say, "Well done, good and faithful servant." As part of Your church, I declare myself subject to Christ. As the wife of my husband, I declare myself subject to his authority as well. I humble myself under Your mighty hand, and the protective authority you have placed over me in the form of my husband. I cast all my care upon You, not him. Thank You that You care for me. Exalt me in Your timing. I pray this in the name of Jesus Christ, amen.

Su M Tu W Th F Sa